Favorite Bible Characters

Copyright © 2000 Scandinavia Publishing House
Drejervej 11-21, DK 2400 Copenhagen NV, Denmark
Tel.: (+45) 35310330 Fax: (+45) 35310334
E-Mail: jvo@scanpublishing.dk

Text copyright © 2000 Marlee Alex, Anne de Graaf, Ben Alex
Illustration copyright © 2000 José Pérez Montero, Philippe Pauzin, Ruth Imhoff, Juan Ramón Alonso, Tiziana Gironi, Alfonso Ruano, Florence Magnin, François Davot, Charles Barat
Produced by Scandinavia Publishing House

Printed in China
ISBN 9788771323948

Favorite BIBLE CHARACTERS

Outstanding Men and Women
of the Bible

By
Marlee Alex
Anne de Graaf
Ben Alex

SCANDINAVIA

INTRODUCTION

Who are the characters of the Bible? Living heroes for today's children. From Moses to Miriam, Peter and Paul to Samuel and Sarah, each of these men and women are real-life role models for this world's young and old.

In *Favorite Bible Characters* children can hear Hannah as she pours her heart out to God, join Joseph as he struggles with the betrayal of his brothers, dare the lions with Daniel, and run with Ruth as she accepts the challenges of a new homeland.

They are all here, eight men and eight women, the strong and the weak, the leaders and the followers, all people seeking God . . . and finding Him in unexpected places.

Dramatic illustrations combine with an active text to make these age-old stories spring off the pages and into the hearts of children and adults. *Favorite Bible Characters* combines sixteen books into one, a treasure for any family library.

Anne de Graaf

TABLE OF CONTENTS

SARAH

A Woman
Whose Dream Came True

By Marlee Alex

Illustrated by Charles Barat

SARAH

A Woman Whose Dream Came True

By Marlee Alex

Illustrated by Charles Barat

Sarah!"
Abraham was still in the distance. Sarah put her needlework aside and went to the tent door. Abraham came running with a big dust cloud at his heels.

"Sarah! Sarah, God spoke to me out in the hills!" Abraham was out of breath. "God said I am going to be a father after all. He said our children will be a blessing to the whole world. That means it's not too late for us to have a baby. You will be a mother, Sarah!"

Abraham paused for breath. He had run all the way from the sloping mountainside and followed the long dusty path back home to his wife.

The tent was snuggled under a mighty oak tree. Branches stretched out over their fire and sleeping mats. This was not the first time Abraham came home to Sarah saying that God had spoken to him and promised them a child. But a long time had passed since the last time.

Sarah felt bubbly inside once again. "Oh, Abraham, I haven't given up hope for that child. And if anyone can recognize the voice of God, you can. I know you listen to God. I'm glad I married you."

Sarah and Abraham had been married many years, but no children had been born to make them the kind of family Sarah dreamed about. Not once had she watched her tummy grow with a baby. Not once had she ever felt tiny thumps and kicks from the inside. Sarah cried many times as month after month passed. She wanted to be a mother, but that seemed like something that happened only in fairy tales.

Sometimes Sarah daydreamed about it. She would dream about the "ga-ga" sounds of a baby at her breast or about a laughing child playing at her feet. Abraham knew what she was thinking about when he saw that faraway look on her face. But he could not make her dream come true. He felt sorry too. Often, he prayed about having a child as he walked in the hills with the herds of oxen and flocks of sheep.

On warm evenings, Sarah and Abraham slept side by side under the stars outside their tent. They loved to watch shooting stars fall across the black sky at bedtime. Once Sarah had tried to count the stars, but there were all too many of them. The stars became a dusty blur. Stardust seemed to fall into her eyes all too soon and she fell fast asleep.

Sarah and Abraham had once lived in a different country called Haran. One day Abraham came home and said, "We're leaving!"

"What, leaving?" Sarah asked.

"Yes, God told us to take a trip!"

"What do you want me to pack, winter clothes or summer clothes?"

Abraham's reply shocked Sarah: "Pack both," he announced. "We re leaving. We 11 never come back to Haran."

So Sarah and Abraham left their family and friends behind. God had told them

to go to the land of Canaan. Sarah sorted through all their clothes and furniture She gave away everything they would not be needing. But she kept one thing that was too precious to leave behind. It was a secret.

"Maybe I will need this someday," she said to herself.

Now, under the mighty oak at Marah in Canaan, Sarah lifted the small box from its hiding place. Abraham was outside washing up. Sarah opened the box and took out one of the baby gowns folded inside. She had sewn the gowns herself. They were made of white linen, embroidered with colored thread and trimmed with lace. Sarah was glad she had brought them with her to Canaan. Now God had spoken again to Abraham about the child he had promised.

"I'm going to be needing these one day," she mused.

Abraham's voice broke her thoughts. "Sarah, we 11 be moving on tomorrow," he said "This isn't the place we're supposed to settle down."

Sarah was getting used to breaking camp and packing up. "Well, it will be nice when we do find the right place," she called back cheerfully.

Once again, they packed up and travelled southward The long train of camels, donkeys, sheep, oxen and all the servants of Abraham made its way slowly through the hills of Canaan. They often stopped to rest. The animals were allowed to graze where the grass was high. The children of the servants splashed in cool streams and pools. Abraham and Sarah took time to worship God. God had called them to Canaan and they were certain he would guide them along the way.

But after weeks of travel the barrels of dried food they had brought along began to look empty. The fresh fruits they had eaten along the way became difficult to find. The green hills of Canaan turned rocky and dry

Abraham's servants began to complain. "We're getting hungry," they cried.

So Abraham had to make a decision "Let's go east!" he told them "I've heard there is plenty of food and water in the land of Egypt."

But there was one problem Egypt was a strong country. Abraham was carrying lots of silver and gold with him. He was afraid the Egyptians would try to rob him. Perhaps they would even try to kill him. Abraham tried to think of ways to make friends with the Egyptians.

Sarah was riding on ahead of Abraham She sat straight and tall on her camel. Her lovely silhouette against the blue sky gave Abraham an idea Many other men had admired Sarah because she was very beautiful. Many times Abraham had seen them glance sidewards at her as she passed by in villages or watering places.

Abraham rode up beside Sarah. "Sarah, you are lovely " he said. "You are bound to be noticed by the men in Egypt. I've been worrying about something The Egyptians might try to kill me in order to get you for a wife If that happened then God would not be able to keep his promise to us. Sarah, I'm afraid.

Shouldn't we tell the Egyptians that you are my sister, and not let them know that you are my wife) Then we have a hope that they will spare our lives."

"But Abraham, why are you talking like that?" Sarah replied. "You know God doesn't need your help to keep a promise he has made." Sarah was laughing, for she did not think Abraham was serious.

The two of them rode on together in front of the camel train. But when they arrived in Egypt Sarah realized that what Abraham had predicted was true. Heads turned toward her as she rode through towns. The eyes of many a man looked into hers. Talk about her beauty flew from mouth to mouth. Eventually, even Pharaoh, the king of Egypt, heard about her. Pharaoh was a man who was used to getting whatever he wanted, and so he insisted on having Sarah as his wife.

Pharaoh's army rode out to the place where Abraham and Sarah had made camp. Abraham turned to Sarah with fear in his eyes. But Sarah jumped up and hurried out to meet them She thought that they intended to kill Abraham She spoke quietly with the soldiers and then rode away with them. Not one of them turned back after Abraham. He stared after them. He did not know what to think.

The next day several of the soldiers came riding back to Abraham's camp. "Now they are coming to kill me," he thought. But the soldiers were carrying treasure chests and leading herds of animals.

The soldiers rode up and laid the chests at Abraham's feet, bowing before him. "These gifts are from Pharaoh," they announced. "Pharaoh wishes to say thank you and to tell you he is pleased with Sarah." Then the soldiers rode away.

Abraham was stunned. He buried his face in his head scarf. He realized that Sarah must have told them that she was his sister anyway. Then Pharaoh would not have to kill Abraham to get her as a wife Abraham felt sad and sorry. 'God, help me get Sarah back," he prayed.

And God did! That day God sent a terrible sickness upon Pharaoh and upon everyone who lived in his house, except Sarah. That made Pharaoh realize that he had done something wrong by taking Sarah as his wife.

"Go back to your husband!" Pharaoh commanded Sarah. "And get out of Egypt with all your servants and animals. I never want to see you again."

Sarah ran back to Abraham as fast as she could Abraham gathered his company and they all trooped quickly out of Egypt. Everyone was relieved to get back to Canaan again. They managed to find enough to eat, and God continued to tell Abraham that he would protect and bless them. God said he would give all the land of Canaan to their children.

But Abraham and Sarah still did not have a child. Ten years had passed since God had promised the first time Abraham believed God's promise He tried to assure Sarah that God meant to keep it.

One day Sarah admitted to Abraham, "How can I go on believing? God promised us we would have a son and as many grandsons as there are stars! How silly! There are more stars than I can count, but not once has my body ever given a hint that I can bear a child And now I am too old to even dream of it!

`Here Abraham," she continued Tears filled her eyes, but she fought them back. "You may take my servant, Hagar, as your wife She is young and lovely Perhaps God will give you a son through her " With a heart full of sadness Sarah left the tent and hurried away to a distant well to fetch water. There she could be alone and cry out her tears before God himself.

Abraham was sorry when Sarah ran off. But he thought to himself, "Maybe Sarah is right ' So he did what she had suggested. Abraham slept with Sarah's servant, Hagar, as if she was his wife Before the end of a year Hagar gave birth to a baby boy. They named the baby Ishmael. Ishmael and his mother, Hagar, continued to live close to Abraham and Sarah and to serve them as year after year passed.

When Abraham and Sarah were almost 100 years old God spoke to Abraham once more. This time God made a special promise about Sarah. "The name Sarah means 'princess'," he said. "Sarah will be blessed like a princess. She will have children who will grow to be kings. Next year she will give birth to a son. You are to call him Isaac. That means 'laughter'. And I will give this land of Canaan to him and to his sons after him."

This time Abraham did not dare tell Sarah what God had said. He had enough trouble believing the promise himself! But one hot summer afternoon as he and Sarah were sitting in the shade beside their tent, three men came walking over the hills towards their camp. Abraham stepped out to welcome the men. He took a crock of water with him and called back to Sarah, "Go in and mix up a fresh batch of bread for our visitors."

As they approached the tent one of the men asked Abraham, "Where is your wife, Sarah?"

"In the tent," Abraham answered.

"This time next year, you and Sarah will have a baby boy!" another one of them exclaimed.

Sarah was standing inside the tent door, and heard what the man had said. She started to chuckle quietly as she thought to herself, "A ninety-one year old woman like me having a baby? Oh, no! God has had plenty of time, but now it's too late."

The third man's voice interrupted Sarah's thoughts. "Why is Sarah laughing?" he asked.

Sarah knew that he could not possibly have heard her. Suddenly she felt scared and excited at the same time.

The third man continued speaking. "You just wait and see. It will happen just like we said it would," he insisted.

There was a lump in Sarah's throat. She swallowed hard and whispered, "Oh, but I did not laugh." She peeked out of the tent door. The men were already heading-down the dusty road. There was something different about them. Were they holy men? Prophets? God himself?

The months passed by and Sarah could not forget the men or what they had said. Sarah's face was tanned and wrinkled. Her back was crooked with age. Her shoulders were stooped. But now her stomach began to grow. It became bigger and rounder every day. Her long robes flared out in front and fell short of the ground.
Everyone could plainly see that she was expecting a baby, but Sarah was almost afraid to believe it herself.

However, sure enough, within a few months' time, a healthy baby boy was born to Sarah and Abraham. Sarah's heart leapt with joy as she held up his soft little body. "God has made me laugh!" she told everyone. "And everyone who ever hears about this--that an old woman like me can have a child --will laugh with me and be happy!" Sarah's face looked young again and her dim eyes lit up with hope.

Sarah's impossible dream had come true at last. She learned that God always keeps His promises, and that he doesn't need anybody's help to do it. Sarah lived a long time after that and she watched Isaac, the child of her dreams, grow to become a man.

You can find the story of Sarah in the Old Testament
from the book of Genesis, chapters 18-23.

JOSEPH

The Boy Who Learned to Handle His Dreams

By Ben Alex

Illustrated by Philippe Pauzin

JOSEPH

The Boy Who Learned to Handle His Dreams

By Ben Alex

Illustrated by Philippe Pauzin

"Look! Here comes the big dreamer!" Joseph's brothers said scornfully. They had just sat down in the green grass to eat their supper when they caught sight of Joseph.

It was easy to spot Joseph, even from far off, because of his bright-colored robe. Joseph's older brothers did not like their little brother. He was their half brother and much younger than any of them. The other day he had caused trouble when he told their father that his brother Judah had taken a nap while watching the sheep.

Their father, Jacob, seemed to fuss so much over Joseph. He always took Joseph's side because Joseph was the firstborn son of his favorite wife Rachel.

At Joseph's recent birthday their father had given Joseph a beautiful bright-colored robe with pockets and long sleeves. Since then his brothers felt Joseph thought he was too important to take care of the sheep. He stayed at home with his little brother Benjamin, the only other child Rachel had had. They played together all day long, while the older brothers stayed with the sheep. It was a hot and tiring job. They thought Joseph would never grow up to become a real shepherd. He usually sat around and daydreamed. The older brothers felt their little brother was a failure, and they did not know what to do about it.

Besides, Joseph talked too much. The brothers hated his bragging. He always seemed to be dreaming about something big. Even their father had to correct him sometimes.

Last week Joseph had told them about a dream he had. "Listen," he had said. "I had a dream last night. I dreamed we all were binding bundles of wheat in the field.

Suddenly my bundle rose while your bundles gathered around mine and bowed down to it. Isn't that interesting?"

The next morning Joseph had described yet another dream. "Listen, brothers! I dreamed that the sun and the moon and eleven stars bowed down to me. Isn't that interesting?"

The brothers did not think so.

Reuben was especially worried about his little brother. Reuben was the eldest of the brothers. He looked forward to being head of the family some day when their father died. Even though he sometimes worried that Joseph might prevent that from happening, he still cared for his little brother.

Reuben shaded his eyes with his hand and watched Joseph running towards them. Then he turned to his brothers. "Listen, I have an idea," he said. "Let's teach Joseph a lesson he'll never forget. We'll throw him into the old dried-up well over there." Reuben pointed at the hole in the ground where the brothers had hoped to find water a few moments earlier. A couple of hours in the well might humble his little brother, Reuben thought.

"Great idea!" said Levi.

"Yes," grinned Judah. "That may cool him off"

By now Joseph had reached the brothers. He stopped to catch his breath. "You...are sure...hard to find," he began. "I've been walking all day. Father told me you were at Shechem. When I arrived there a man told me you'd gone on to Dothan. Father told me to find you and report back to him how you're doing with the sheep. I'm sure glad that..."

Before Joseph could finish, Judah and Simeon grabbed his arms and held him while the other brothers tied up his arms.

"Hey listen!" yelled Joseph. "I'm your brother! Judah, get off my toes! What are you...? Aghh I" A big hand over Joseph's mouth finally silenced him. His eyes bulged as he started to realize what his brothers were doing.

The brothers threw Joseph down into the dark well.

At first Joseph could see nothing at all. But gradually, as his eyes got used to the dark, he could see the stone walls rising round him. The floor was slimy and clammy. He shivered. He hated snakes and scorpions and lizards. About ten feet above his head he could see his brothers' heads against the sky in the narrow opening.

"Dream yourself some great dreams down there!" grinned Levi. Then the heads disappeared and Joseph was left alone.

The brothers finished their meal on the grass near the well. Tonight was Reuben's turn to watch the sheep. After the meal he went off to the field and left the brothers at the well.

"I watch the sheep. You watch Joseph," he said as he left.

Before long, Judah saw dust clouds far way. A caravan slowly approached them from the north. "I've got an idea," he whispered. "Why not sell Joseph to the caravan merchants? Then we'll get rid of him."

The others agreed.

"Slave for sale! Slave for sale!" From the well Joseph heard the shouting. He could also hear the hoofbeats of camels and donkeys.

"They're going to sell me!" he gasped.

"They're really going to sell me! We're not playing games anymore! Father! I wish Father were here!"

But Joseph's father was far away, at home in Mamre at Hebron. There was no way he

could hear his favorite son's cry for help. And Reuben was not there to stop the brothers' plan.

So, Joseph was sold by his brothers to the merchants. "He seems to be a strong and handsome boy," said the merchants. "We'll pay you twenty pieces of silver for him."

Then the caravan left with Joseph. When Reuben returned from the pastures he realized what had happened. "Are you crazy?' he yelled. 'What are we supposed to do now? How will you explain this to Father?"

All the way home the brothers tried to come up with an answer. Finally, they decided to kill a goat and smear the blood on Joseph s bright-colored robe. They would tell their father Joseph was killed by a wild animal in the wilderness.

Father Jacob wept for many days when he heard the story of Joseph's death. "My poor son is dead," he mourned. "I shall cry till the day I die."

In the meantime, Joseph arrived in Egypt Night after night he had cried himself to sleep on the dusty caravan trail, not knowing what was going to happen to him. He knew he had been sold as a slave. He also knew how slaves were usually treated.

Some were put to work in the horrible copper mines There they worked every day, nonstop. Most of those slaves died in the mines. Others became oarsmen on the Egyptian battleships Most of those soon drowned or were killed. Others became brick-makers or metalworkers. They were whipped and tortured. Joseph would never be a free man again. The rest of his life, though probably very short, would be spent doing nothing but endless, tedious chores.

Joseph shivered at the thought of it.

Now the caravan entered a huge city in Egypt. For a moment Joseph forgot about his hopeless future. When they crossed the Nile River, the fantastic pyramids of Egypt rose in front of him. He had never seen anything like it! He was used to tents and sheep. This was wonderful! The majestic buildings, the crowded streets, the beautiful sculptures, the enormous pyramids! It was another world, even more exciting than the world of his childhood dreams!

"Hey, you... come here!"

Joseph was startled back into remembering why he was there. The merchant dragged him to a nearby marketplace. There he spoke to a big fat Egyptian, but Joseph could not understand what they said. Then the Egyptian placed Joseph on a little platform in the street, together with some other slaves. The fat Egyptian shouted and made all kinds of gestures to attract people's attention. Joseph guessed he shouted the same words his brothers had shouted at the well at Dothan, "Slave for sale!"

Joseph was sold to a wealthy Egyptian named Potiphar. He was an important man. He was the captain of King Pharaoh s bodyguard. He looked stern and kind at the same time. Joseph soon learned that Potiphar meant to use him as a house servant. He would not have to waste away in the copper mines! Joseph sighed in relief "Thank You God," he whispered. 'I know You will watch over me!'

Joseph worked faithfully for Potiphar. He even worked harder than he was asked to. One day Potiphar said to Joseph, Joseph! I'm very pleased with the work you do. You are a skilled and honest young man. It seems like you have the favor of our gods."

"The God of Abraham, Isaac and Jacob is with me," answered Joseph.

"Anyway,' continued Potiphar, "I think I'll put you in charge of my entire household. From now on you shall be called my steward."

Now Joseph was free to walk all over Potiphar's property. He was given a beautiful new cloak. He made sure his master had his meals served on time. He ordered the food and made sure the house was neat and clean. Joseph took pride in managing Potiphar's household. And in doing this, he was taking the credit for his luck instead of seeing it as a blessing from God.

One day, when Joseph was walking down the hall past the bedroom of Potiphar's wife, she approached him. "Joseph, why don't you come and sleep with me tonight? My husband is out of town."

Joseph knew this was wrong. How could he do such a thing when his master trusted him? Joseph ran down the hallway before Potiphar's wife could touch him. But the woman ran after him and managed to pull off his cloak.

Now she wanted to hurt Joseph because he had not done what she wanted So, when Potiphar came home she lied. "My dear husband, something terrible happened while you were away. Joseph, your Hebrew slave, tried to force me to sleep with him. See, here's the cloak he left behind in my bedroom."

Potiphar believed her lies.

"Put this wicked Joseph in prison!" he told one of his soldiers. "Because he has done this, he will spend the rest of his life behind bars!"

As the heavy iron door slammed shut behind Joseph and the key turned in the lock, Joseph sat down on the wet and filthy floor and cried. Now he was back where he had started, and there was no way to get out.

"God," he sobbed, "why am I so unlucky? I've lost my family, my country, and now my job in Potiphar's house. Are You still with me? I trust You, Lord. I trust You'll somehow find a way to get me out."

In the dark prison Joseph did not dream at all. He realized he had put his trust in himself and not in God's faithfulness. "I am sorry, God," he prayed. "Help me to forget myself and my big ambitions. Help me to serve You .. . even in this horrible place."

So, Joseph began to serve the prisoners around him. Many of them were sick. He brought them water and helped them clean up their cells. He tried to comfort them with a few cheerful words and a smile Everybody in prison liked him, and soon the prison warden gave him little jobs to do. "Joseph," he said, "I see you

care for other people. I like that. Besides, I feel I can trust you. Your God must be with you in a special way. From now on you shall be overseer of the prisoners."

Among the other prisoners were two very important ones. One was King Pharaoh's former baker. The other had been in charge of filling Pharaoh's wine cup. Pharaoh had thrown them in prison because he did not trust them anymore. One morning when Joseph visited their cell they both looked very sad.

"What's wrong with you two?" asked Joseph cheerfully "Did you have nightmares?"

"Actually," they answered, "we both had strange dreams last night, and we have no idea what they could mean."

"Oh," answered Joseph. Then he thought for a moment before he said, "Why not let God Himself interpret your dreams?"

"God?" asked the cup bearer doubtfully.

"How can God do that?"

"Well," said Joseph. "Tell me your dreams. Maybe God will tell you through me."

"I dreamed," said the cup bearer, that I saw a vine in front of me The vine had three branches. Buds popped out and the these-buds blossomed right away. Then clusters grew on the branches and the grapes ripened. The next thing I noticed was Pharaoh's cup in my hand. I took the grapes, squeezed them into the cup and put the cup in the king's hand."

"All right," said Joseph, "here's what your dream means. The three branches mean three days Within three days King Pharaoh will release you from the prison and make you his cup bearer again. Now do you have any reason to look so sad?"

"Wonderful!" the man shouted. "Joseph, I like the way you explained my dream! I only wish I could do something for you in return."

Joseph looked serious. "You can," he said. "You can tell Pharaoh about me. I've done nothing wrong. Yet my life is wasting away in this prison. Maybe Pharaoh will let me go"

"I promise!" answered the cup bearer.

Now it was the baker's turn to tell Joseph about his dream. "I dreamed," he said, "there were three baskets piled on top of my head. In the top basket were all kinds of cakes and bread I had made for Pharaoh. Suddenly the birds came and ate the cakes and the bread."

Joseph felt sorry for the baken when he explained his dream. "This is what your dream means," he said. "The three baskets mean three days. Within three days Pharaoh will hang you by your neck, and the birds shall come and eat your flesh."

Three days later it happened exactly as Joseph had said it would. The cup bearer was back at his old job. The baker was killed.

But two years passed and Joseph still did not get out of prison. The cup bearer had forgotten his promise.

One morning as the cup bearer filled Pharaoh's cup with wine, he noticed the king did not look well. "Is anything wrong, your Majesty?" he asked.

Pharaoh sighed. I had two strange dreams last night," he answered. "I'm going to call all the wise men of Egypt, tell them about my dreams, and see if they can explain them to me."

But the wise men could not give Pharaoh any answers. They just stood there, the priests, the fortune-tellers, the dream Interpreters and the magicians. They looked so important in their beautiful robes, yet all they could say was, "Strange!"

"Peculiar!"

"Interesting!"

Then the cup bearer remembered Joseph. "Your Majesty, ' he interrupted, "in the prison there is a Hebrew slave who once told me the meaning of a dream I had. Maybe he can explain your dreams."

So Joseph was commanded to appear before Pharaoh.

"I've heard about you," said Pharaoh. You're supposed to be good at interpreting dreams. Now tell me what my dreams mean."

"Your Majesty," answered Joseph, "I cannot interpret dreams. But God can."

"Anyway,' continued Pharaoh, "here's what I dreamed. I was standing on the banks of the River Nile. Out of the river came seven fat cows. They began to graze on the banks. Then seven thin cows came up and ate the seven fat cows. Afterwards I had another dream. I saw a grain stalk with seven good and healthy heads of grain on it. Then seven other heads of grain sprouted on it. But they were thin and scorched by the east wind. Finally the thin heads of grain swallowed up the seven good heads. Now tell me the meaning of these things!"

Joseph looked at Pharaoh. He took a deep breath. Pharaoh looked so frightening as he sat on his throne, impatiently waiting for Joseph to answer. What did the dreams mean? Would God tell Joseph?

Joseph cleared his throat and began to speak 'Pharaoh's two dreams...mean... the

same thing. God wants to tell you what is going to happen soon. The seven fat cows and the seven healthy heads of grain mean seven years. The seven thin cows and the seven thin heads of grain mean another seven years. God is warning you that after seven good years with bountiful crops and plenty to eat, there will come seven bad years with scant crops and severe famine in Egypt.

"Pharaoh ought to find a trustworthy and wise man to put in charge of the royal storehouses This man must make sure enough food from the seven good years are stored so the people of Egypt can have enough to survive the seven bad years."

"Excellent idea!" exclaimed Pharaoh. "Young man, what's your name?"

"Joseph, your Majesty"

"Joseph," continued Pharaoh, "I will appoint you the new manager of my storehouses since you are the one who told me the meaning of my dreams. Your God must be with you in a special way!"

When Joseph walked away, he still could not believe Pharaoh's words How could things happen so fast? After all those years in prison he had suddenly become the second- most-important man in Egypt, next to Pharaoh himself!

But Joseph did not fully realize that when God raises a man to honor and responsibility, He does not do it overnight. It takes time. For Joseph it took many years. Joseph was a good man who had learned to honor God for His blessings.

More than thirteen years had passed since the day Joseph was thrown in the well by his brothers. In that time he had become the governor of Egypt, second only to Pharaoh. He wore the royal signet ring, and when he drove his royal chariot through the streets, people bowed to him and called him "Sire."

And it had happened exactly as Joseph had foretold. First came the seven good years with plenty to eat. Joseph had stored millions of tons of grain in the royal storehouses for the bad years to come. Then, despite the years of famine there was enough food for the people in Egypt. But the countries around Egypt suffered greatly.

Back in the land of Canaan Jacob and his sons had barely enough to eat. The grass was gone. The wells had dried up. Jacob's green fields had become desert.

Every day Jacob's sons came home with worse news than the day before. "Forty more sheep died today!' reported Reuben one day. "I'm sorry Father, but this can t go on."

"Well, don't just stand there!" scolded Jacob "Do something! Why don't you go to Egypt? I told you there's food in Egypt. I heard it from a caravan last month Go and buy some grain before we die like the sheep in the field. Hurry up! But, in case something should happen to you, I don't want Benjamin to get hurt. Benjamin stays home with me!"

When the ten brothers arrived at the storehouses of Egypt, they were brought before the governor, who was Joseph. Of course they did not recognize their little brother. He had become a man. He wore beautiful clothes. He looked like a prince. Even his name had been changed from Joseph to Zaphenath-paneah They bowed before him and told him about the famine in the land of Canaan.

But Joseph recognized his brothers. As they bowed down before him, he remembered the dreams he had dreamt as a child. But he decided not to reveal who he was. He even pretended he did not understand his brothers' language. Everything they said had to be translated into the Egyptian language.

“I don't believe you,” he replied harshly when the brothers had told their story. He wanted to test them. “I think you are spies from the land of Canaan. You intend to bring an army against Egypt, and that's why you have come disguised as farmers!”

“Your Honor,” said Simeon, “that's not true! We have come to Egypt to buy grain We are brothers, not spies. Our father sent us”

“No,” repeated Joseph. “You are spies!”

“Sir,” pleaded Simeon, “I assure you we tell the truth! Our father sent us to buy grain.”

“Who is your father then?”

“Our father is Jacob, also called Israel, from Hebron in the land of Canaan. He had twelve sons. One of them is dead, the other one stayed home with him. We are the remaining ten sons.”

“Hmm,” said Joseph, “we'll see whether you speak the truth or not.”

Then he had the ten brothers put in prison for three days. “I want them to know what an Egyptian prison is like,” he thought to himself.

After three days he told the ten brothers, "I've made my decision. You may buy grain and take it back to Canaan. But I want to put you to the test in order to see if you spoke the truth. I will keep one of you in prison as a hostage while the other nine of you go home and bring your little brother back to me."

At Joseph's words Simeon turned to his brothers. "Oh no," he said in their own language, thinking Joseph could not under-

stand. "Father will never allow that. I think we're in trouble. We are getting what we deserve. God is punishing us because we sold Joseph as a slave. Do you remember how he cried out when we sold him for twenty silver pieces? But we didn't listen. We can thank ourselves for the mess we're in now."

"Yes," said Reuben, the oldest brother. "Didn't I tell you it was wrong? Why didn't you listen to me?"

"Please Reuben," interrupted Simeon.

"You've said that a thousand times. You go back to our father with the rest of our brothers and ask to bring Benjamin back with you. I'll stay here as the governor's hostage."

Joseph listened while his brothers talked. He found it difficult to hold back his tears. He felt pity and sorrow for his brothers. Of course he had understood every word they said. He hurried outside and wept by himself. Now he knew his brothers felt sorry for what they had done.

But still, he did not let them know who he was. First he wanted to see his little brother Benjamin.

Father Jacob was angry when he heard their message. "Why did you even tell the Egyptian governor you had another brother at home?" he shouted at his sons. "You want to go back to Egypt and take Benjamin, my dead Rachel's Benjamin, with you? I can never let that happen!"

"But Father," said Reuben, "we must go back! Simeon is being held hostage in Egypt. The governor will not release him unless we bring Benjamin. I promise you, we will bring Benjamin safely back to you. You may take my own two sons if we don't!"

"Look!" Levi interrupted them. He was unpacking the donkeys with the sacks of grain from Egypt "Here's the money purse which I gave in return for the grain, lying right on top!"

"My money is here, too!" shouted his brother Gad. Now the other brothers untied their sacks. On top of each sack of grain was the money they were supposed to have paid for it.

"I don't understand this!" said Reuben.

Even though the nine brothers wanted to return"I'm sure we paid. What will the governor of Egypt think when he realizes we brought our money back with us? He may punish Simeon for it! Father, we have to go back to Egypt and take Benjamin with them, Jacob was firm "No!" he commanded. He knew he may never see Simeon again, but he would not trade Benjamin for Simeon.

A year passed. Finally Jacob realized he had no choice. He would have to send his sons back to Egypt to buy more grain. One morning after all the grain had been eaten and they had been starving for days, Jacob said to his sons, "Go back to Egypt and buy more grain."

"All right Father," answered Judah, "but you know we have to take Benjamin along with us. The governor may kill all of us if we show up without him."

"I'll give you plenty of money to pay for the grain," retorted Jacob.
"We still must take Benjamin with us," repeated Judah.

"Very well," sighed Jacob. "But no harm must come to him! Take a double amount of silver with you to pay for both the new grain and the grain you got last time. Here, take these gifts for the governor as well, balm, honey, myrrh and spices.. . and pistachio nuts and almonds."

So the brothers trudged back down to Egypt once again.

And this time Benjamin went with them.

Joseph, the governor, greeted them sternly. "What took you so long? Is this the youngest brother?"

Joseph looked carefully at the newcomer. He knew it was Benjamin! Oh, how he had missed his little brother! He wanted to hug him and tell him who he was. He wanted to kiss him and talk to him like in the old days. But he dared not, not yet.

Instead he invited his brothers to eat with him in his own house, still not revealing who he was.

"How is your father?" Joseph asked the brothers at the table. "Is he still alive?"

So they told him about their aged father and the trouble they all were in because of the famine in Canaan. While they were eating and speaking, Joseph thought of a plan.

The next morning he told his servants to load the brothers' donkeys with food. "Now listen carefully," he continued to his servant. "Put each man's silver on top of the grain just like the last time. Then take my precious silver cup and lay it together with the money in the youngest brother's sack."

"But. .. " said the servant.

"Just do exactly as I say," commanded Joseph.

On their way back to Canaan the brothers were happy and cheerful. Both Benjamin and Simeon were with them. They sang and joked as they drove their loaded donkeys north toward Hebron.

"Great fellow, this governor, huh?" shouted Judah.

"Yes," Reuben shouted back. "He's not as tough as I thought?"

"Did you know," said Levi, who was the cleverest one of them all, "most Egyptians would never dream of eating with a Hebrew? Still, the governor invited us to eat at his very own table!"

"I even began to like him," laughed Reuben.

Suddenly, as one of the brothers turned around, he noticed a dust cloud on the horizon behind them. The cloud slowly grew. They realized they were being followed by Egyptian soldiers. The soldiers caught up with them, jumped off their horses and commanded, "Stop in the name of Pharaoh!"

"What's the matter?" protested Reuben. He stepped between the soldiers and the brothers.

"The governor's silver cup has disappeared," answered the captain in charge. "The governor has sent us to see ifone of you stole it."

"Stole it?" exclaimed Reuben. "I assure you...."

"Open your bags!" interrupted the captain. He had the brothers stand in a long line, Reuben first, Benjamin last. When he came to Benjamin he dug his arm down into the sack and triumphantly raised the sparkling silver cup over his head.

"Oh no," said Judah. "Benjamin stole the governor's silver cup! I can't believe it!"

"Benjamin!" said Reuben. "What have you done?"

But Benjamin just stared at the silver cup. He had no idea how it had ended up in his sack.

"You are under arrest!" said the captain, grabbing Benjamin by the shoulder. Then he turned to the other brothers. "You must all follow me back to the governor's house," he said.

So they loaded their donkeys again, turned around and went slowly back to the city.

Joseph was waiting at home for his brothers to be brought back. By putting the silver cup in Benjamin's sack he had made sure he had a good reason to arrest Benjamin. He intended to let the other brothers go home and keep only Benjamin, his dear little brother.

"What have you done to me?" he said sternly to the brothers standing in front of him. "You. .. yes you. .. Benjamin, you stole my silver cup!"

Benjamin trembled. He had not done it. He knew that. How could the governor's silver cup have ended up in his sack? Benjamin noticed the way the governor pronounced his name. For a fraction of a second it reminded him of his lost brother Joseph, with whom he had played in the fields of Hebron as a small boy.

"I'm putting your youngest brother under arrest!" continued the governor. "He'll be a slave in Egypt for the rest of his life. But all of you are free to go back to your country."

"Your Honor," Judah cried, "allow me to speak a word. If Benjamin doesn't return with us, our father will die from sorrow. He cannot bear to lose his youngest son. He has already lost one. Please let me take Benjamin's place and be your slave instead." Joseph looked at his brothers. They were all in tears. Tears appeared in his own eyes. He bit his lip trying to control his expression, but it was no use.
"Servants," he commanded, "leave me alone with these Hebrew men!"

The tears rolled down his cheeks as he stepped closer and took off his Egyptian headdress.

"Joseph!" gasped Benjamin.

"Benjamin!" wept Joseph as he hugged his younger brother. Then Joseph went from brother to brother and named them by their Hebrew names as he kissed them. For a long time no words were spoken, but the weeping of the twelve united brothers was heard throughout the governor's house.

Finally Joseph said, "Brothers, do not regret what you did to me when you sold me as a slave many years ago. God has been with me and turned my troubles into a blessing. How I've longed to share my blessings with you. Now, go back to our father and to your families and bring them down to Egypt. Yes, and bring all your possessions and cattle and sheep. I will prepare a place for you with plenty of grain and water. I want you to beguests of Pharaoh and Egypt."

Joseph's childhood dreams had come true. He had become the most powerful man in the world, next to King Pharaoh himself. He had become so mighty, even his own brothers had bowed before him.

But not only had Joseph's dreams come true. God's purpose for him came true as well. Through Joseph's faithfulness when times were hard, and his endurance in prison, Joseph had learned to see that his blessings came from God. In this way he became a man capable of handling his big dreams. He had become a man of compassion and humility, able to forget himself and reach out to those around him.

So, when Joseph's father finally came to Egypt and bowed before his son, Joseph pulled him to his feet and hugged him.

"Welcome, Father!" he whispered.

You can find the story of Joseph in the Old Testament in the book of Genesis, chapters 37–50.

MOSES

God's Chosen Leader

By Anne de Graaf

Illustrated by José Pérez Montero

MOSES

God's Chosen Leader

By Anne de Graaf

Illustrated by José Pérez Montero

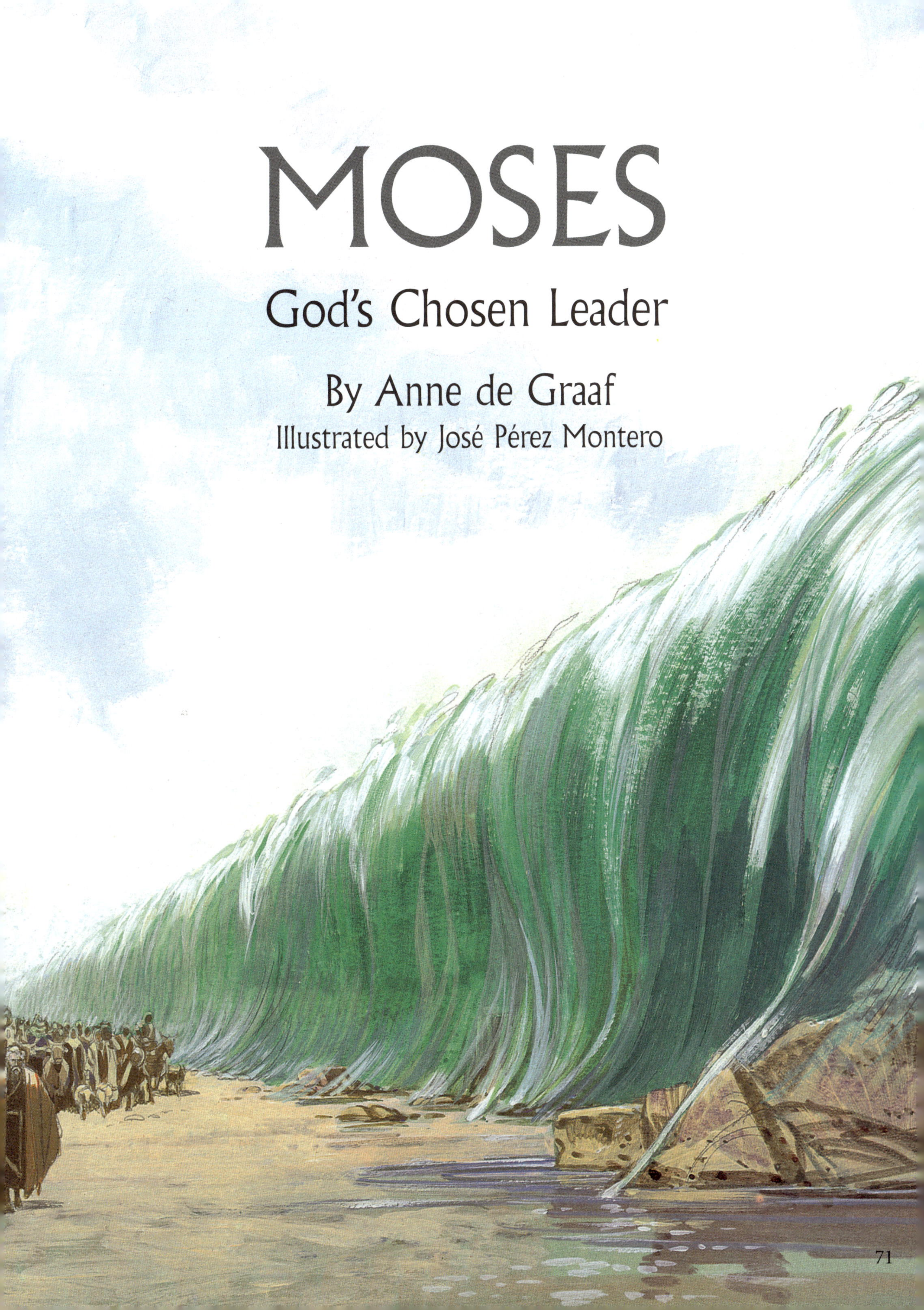

A very, very long time ago, a special little baby boy was born. He lived in Egypt. His family was not Egyptian, though. They were Hebrews, or Israelites.

The Israelites had come to Egypt hundreds of years before this baby was born. At that time the Egyptians had made them welcome. But in the hundreds of years since then, there had been many Israelites born. Now the Egyptians were afraid of the Israelites, so they made them into slaves!

This meant that when this baby was born, his mother had to hide him. The pharaoh, or Egyptian king, had ordered all Israelite boys to be killed! Only the girls could live, and only if they worked as slaves.

All babies are beautiful. This one was extra special. "I just know in my heart, he will grow up to be someone great," his mother told her two older children.

The one brother was named Aaron. He had not been killed by the soldiers. Now the family asked God to protect this second son as well. "Please show us a way to save him," they prayed. They were not afraid of the pharaoh. And then they thought of a plan.

When the pharaoh's soldiers were not looking, the family brought the baby to the great River Nile. They wrapped him in his favorite blanket and placed him into a basket. Then the mother said a prayer, "Lord, please don't let our son drown or be found by the Egyptian soldiers!"

Down the river floated the baby! The quiet lapping of the waves rocked him slowly to sleep.

"A baby! Look everyone! It's a baby in a basket!" The pharaoh's daughter had come to the river for a swim. When she saw the basket floating down the river, though, she had told a servant to bring it to her. Now she looked down at the baby and said, "Oh, poor thing. He must be one of the Hebrew children." She felt sorry for the child. "Look how he's sucking his hand. He's hungry!"

The baby's sister had followed the basket down the river. Now she stepped forward. "Shall I ask one of the Hebrew women to nurse him for you?" She meant her mother, of course.

"Yes, that would be good for him," the princess said. "I will make this boy my own. Tell the soldiers that if they bother you. When he's old enough to eat solid food, bring him to the palace. He will grow up as my son."

His real mother was overjoyed to welcome the child back home. The family thanked God for answering their prayers. Yes, this certainly was a very special baby.

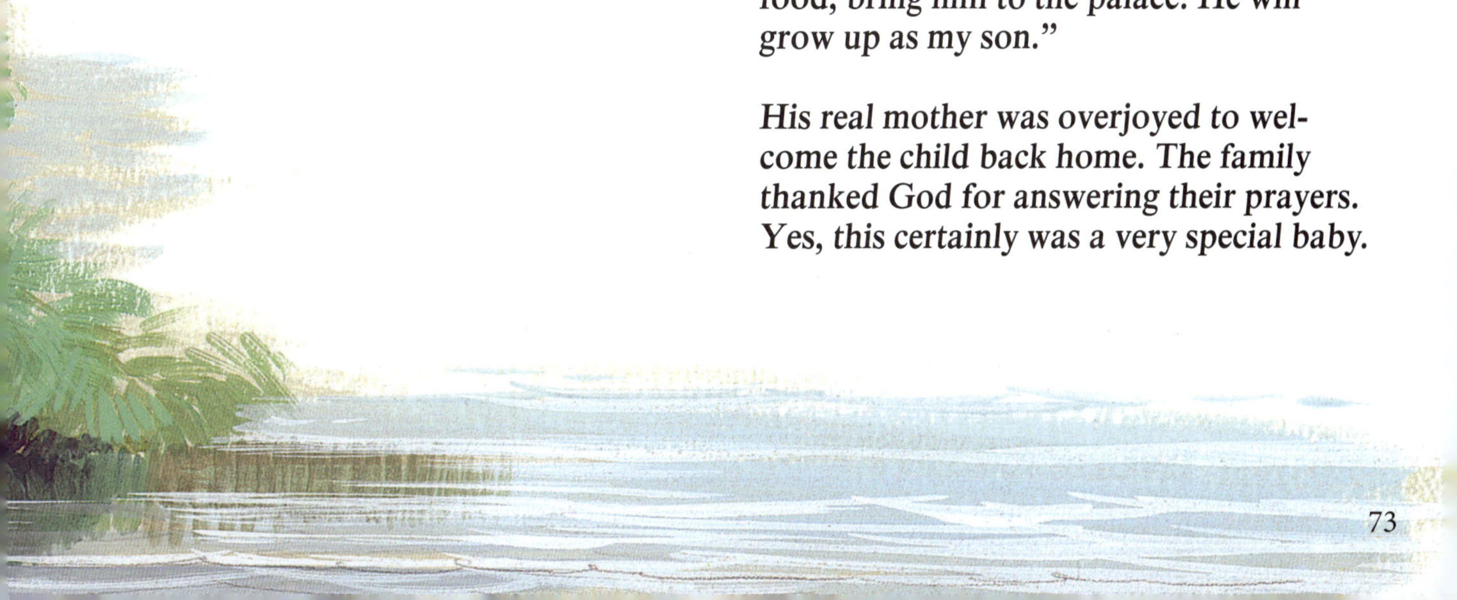

A year or so later his sister brought the baby to the princess. "Oh, look at how cute he is!" The pharaoh's daughter took the baby into her arms. "I will call him Moses. That's a good name, don't you think so?"

Moses' sister smiled. She knew her little brother was in good hands. She went home and together with her parents, prayed for Moses. At least now he would not have to grow up as a slave.

The princess did take good care of Moses. She loved him and gave him the best of everything. As Moses grew older he learned all about the history of Egypt. He also learned about his own group of people, the Hebrews.

"But why are all the Hebrews slaves?" he asked his mother.

"Because the pharaoh needs workers. He needs people to take care of the fields and build the pyramids."

"But it's not fair!" young Moses cried. "I've seen the Egyptians whip my people. Sometimes they don't even have enough to eat!"

His adopted mother looked away. "Yes, I know, Moses. But there's nothing we can do about it. Remember why you are a prince. My father, your grandfather, is the mighty pharaoh. We must all do as he says."

Moses thought, "I will do something! It's not right. My history teachers told me the Hebrews came here to work with the Egyptians, not for them!"

Years went by and in that time Moses also learned there was a difference between the Egyptian gods, which were not real, and the God of the Hebrews, who is very real.

When Moses was about forty years old he finally had a chance to do something for his people. One day, he was walking home to the palace when he turned a corner and saw an Egyptian beating up a Hebrew slave!

Moses could not hold himself back. "You there!" he ran toward the man. "This is the last time you ever hit one of my people!" The Egyptian looked up in surprise. Moses hit him as hard as he could. Over and over they tumbled in the sand. Then Moses killed the Egyptian. As fast as he could, Moses buried the body so no one would find it.

The next day Moses saw two slaves fighting. "Stop this!" he pulled them apart. "You should be fighting the Egyptians, not each other."

"Who do you think you are?" they turned on Moses. "We saw you kill that Egyptian yesterday!"

Moses gasped, "You know!"

"Who doesn't?" the two slaves laughed at Moses.

Moses ran for his life.

Moses left Egypt and his life as a prince far behind. Moses ran deep, deep into the desert. The pharaoh's guards came back empty-handed. Moses had disappeared without a trace. Or had he?

Once Moses knew he was safe, he asked himself, "I've run away, but now what do I do? I don't know how to find food in the desert. What if I die?" A few days later Moses found a well.

There he saw several shepherds who would not let some women get their water.
Moses chased away the bullies. When he helped the women, they invited him home for a meal.

The women were sisters. Their father was a wise man belonging to a tribe which traveled through the desert. They lived in tents and kept sheep. Moses became a good friend of the father. He married one of the daughters and spent the next forty years working as a shepherd.

During that time Moses learned that he was not the important prince he once had been in Egypt. Out in the desert he was just an ordinary shepherd.

More than once under those huge night skies, Moses mumbled to himself, "There's nothing special about me. All I'm good at is running away." Moses did not like himself very much. Then something happened which changed his life forever.

One day, Moses was at the foot of a mountain, looking for some sheep. They had wandered off among the rocks and high cliffs.

All at once he saw something very strange.

"A fire!" He waited to see which way the fire would spread. Would the wind blow it toward Moses and his flock or away from them? It did neither. The fire stayed in one spot!

Moses could not believe his eyes. He walked closer and a shiver ran up his back. "What's this?" he asked out loud.

The bush was on fire, but did not burn! Inside the fire the bush was still green.

Suddenly, Moses heard a Voice speak out of the flames. "Moses, Moses !"

"Here I am."

The Voice coming from the bush said, "I am the God of your fathers, the God of Abraham, Isaac and Jacob, the God of the Israelites."

As Moses knelt, God said, "I have seen the Egyptians hurt My people all these years. I have heard them crying out for help. I know their pain. Now the time has come for you to lead them out of Egypt. Take them into the land I promised My people so long ago. Speak to Pharaoh. Tell him to let My people go."

Moses shook his head. "But I'm a nothing person," he thought to himself. "I'm only good at running away. Why does God choose a loser like me?"

Out loud, Moses said, "But . . . but why should I be the one to speak to Pharaoh?"

"Because I will be with you. You're My chosen leader."

Moses shuddered. "But . . . I can't! What would I tell them? Who do I say sent me?"

"Tell them the Lord God has sent you," God answered.

Moses felt miserable. "I'm no good," he thought to himself. So he argued with God. He did not want the job. "But . . . but why should they believe me? What sign can I give them that I've been sent by God?"

"When you throw your staff to the ground it will become a snake. When you pick it up again it will become a staff. Try it."

Moses threw his staff on the ground. When it wiggled away as a snake, Moses cried out and ran away. Then Moses stepped over to the snake and picked it up. In his hands it became a wooden staff again.

Moses was afraid. "But . . . but I . . . don't speak well. How am I going to tell the pharaoh that he should set the Hebrews free? He won't listen to me! Please . . . ."

The Lord said to him, "Just go and I will be with you. I will teach you what to say." Moses' fear made him foolish. "Please, please send someone else."

The flames from the bush grew brighter and more fierce. "What about your brother Aaron?" God said. This was the older brother who had prayed with Moses' family when Moses was just a tiny baby.

God said, "He can speak well. I will send him here to meet you. All you have to do is tell him what to say and he will help you. I have chosen you to lead the people, though. Now go!"

Moses hung his head. What more could he say? Moses finally accepted what God had asked of him. Only then did God take care of Moses' fear. He told him, "The pharaoh and his men who were trying to kill you are all dead now. There is another pharaoh. He will not hurt you."

Moses nodded. He felt as if he were taking a big step down a long, dark tunnel. Moses heard in his thoughts God's promise, "I will be with you."

On the way to Egypt, Moses did meet his brother Aaron Moses told him everything that had happened. The brothers traveled the rest of the way together. They were on a mission from God.

"But you must believe us!" Aaron spoke to the Hebrew leaders in Egypt. Every one of the old men at the meeting were slaves. Some were shaking their heads at what Aaron said, "God has chosen Moses to lead you out of Egypt."

Moses stepped forward. He took a deep breath and said, "Watch this. This is the sign we will show Pharaoh so he will let you go!" Moses threw his staff on the floor.

When the staff turned into a snake, everyone gasped, "Yes, they really are from God!"

"We believe! Tell us what to do!"

Aaron said, "Pray for us. Now we give Pharaoh God's message."

As they approached Pharaoh's palace, Moses felt like running away again. He looked at his brother walking next to him Then Moses looked up at the gates. "This is it," he mumbled Moses knew what he had to do.

Once inside the palace, Moses walked down the same halls he had played in as a boy.

"What do you want?" the great and mighty pharaoh of Egypt growled.

"We have a message from the great and mighty God of our fathers. He says you should let all the Hebrew slaves leave Egypt."

Pharaoh laughed. "Ha! A god of slaves! What nonsense, get out of my sight!"

Moses and Aaron looked at each other. This was not going to be easy "The God of the Hebrews says He wants His people to leave Egypt for three days and worship Him."

"Don't be ridiculous!" Pharaoh roared "Slaves can't take a vacation! It's just because you are lazy! The Hebrews work for me and no one else!'

Moses and Aaron had warned the pharaoh. He had chosen not to listen. Even when he saw the staff turn into a snake, Pharaoh said, "That's just a wizard's trick! Look!" At that the kmg's wizards did the same thing with their staffs. They turned into snakes too! But Moses' staff swallowed them up!

Still, Pharaoh did not believe in God. Now God would give Pharaoh ten very good reasons why he should let His people go. God told Moses, "I will send ten plagues to Egypt. After the plagues, all Egyptians, even Pharaoh, will know I am God. Then he will let My people go.

The ten plagues were horrible! First God changed all the water in Egypt into blood. All the fish died. Pharaoh could not take a bath!

Then God sent thousands of frogs. Moses had warned Pharaoh, "God says to let His people go." Pharaoh had not listened. The frogs hopped their way out of the rivers and ponds and into the Egyptians' homes. That's when Pharaoh called Moses.

"Get rid of them! Do whatever you have to, but stop these frogs!"

"God says, 'Let My people go." '

"All right! Yes, tomorrow. They can all leave tomorrow, anything, just get rid of the frogs. They're all over the kitchens and I even found one in my bed!"

When all the frogs had gone, though, Pharaoh changed his mind. "No! The slaves may not go free. I need them to work!"

So God sent swamis of tiny and big flies. They landed on everything. All the animals and people were covered with the creeping, crawling flies. The tiny flies were the worst.

Then God sent a sickness so that all the Egyptians' cattle died. During these last plagues only the Egyptians and their homes were harmed. God was careful to spare the Hebrews and their animals.

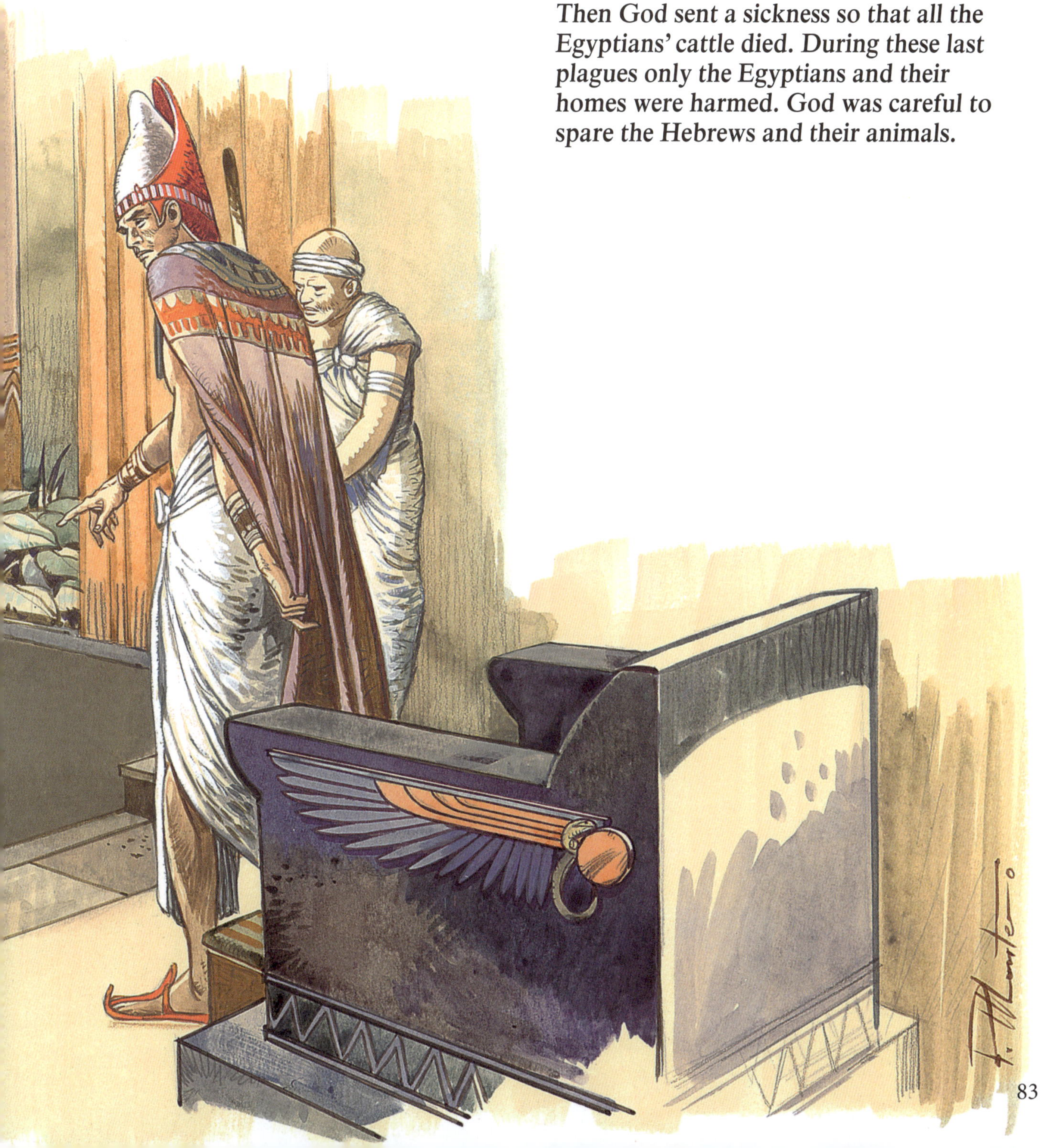

Every time a new plague hit Egypt, Pharaoh sent for Moses. "Make it stop and I'll let the Hebrews go free," he begged. Each time Moses went to the Lord in prayer and God stopped the plague. But then Pharaoh would change his mind, again and again.

God sent a fine dust to fall from the sky. It landed on all the Egyptians' faces, then grew into horrible sores! "Agh! What is wrong with us?" the Egyptians cried.

The Israelites shook their heads There was nothing wrong with their skin. "You should tell your pharaoh to let us go."

The Egyptians pleaded with Pharaoh. Even his own magicians and servants begged him to let the Hebrews go free. "Their God is too strong for us," they said.

Pharaoh shook his head. "They aren't going anywhere but back to work, where they belong!" he boomed.

Then the Lord sent the worst hailstorm Egypt had ever seen. Thunder shook the land as fire and hail fell from the sky Anyone caught outside was killed by the huge hailstones. They were as big as melons! All the plants and grass were crushed flat.

Then God sent a huge cloud of locusts, which ate every green leaf in Egypt. They covered all the ground until it was black. But where the Israelites were living it was light. Pharaoh finally said, "Enough! Take your people and leave us alone!" But then he changed his mind again!

God sent darkness to settle over the land. Day became night and night lasted for days. again Pharaoh told Moses, "Leave

us. Go now! But make sure you leave your sheep and cattle behind." He was very angry and once again, Pharaoh changed his mind He still would not let God's people go.

Finally, the Lord said to Moses, "I will bring one more plague on Egypt. After that Pharaoh will let you go. But first you must protect yourselves against what I am about to do."

Moses had learned a great deal while all this was happening. He had learned that God means what He says. Now Moses warned God's people that they should paint their doors with lamb's blood. That night God would cause every eldest son to die in his bed This would happen in most of the Egyptian homes, but not in the homes of the Hebrews. The lamb's blood would protect the Israelites. In the years to come, God's people would always remember that night as the very first Passover.

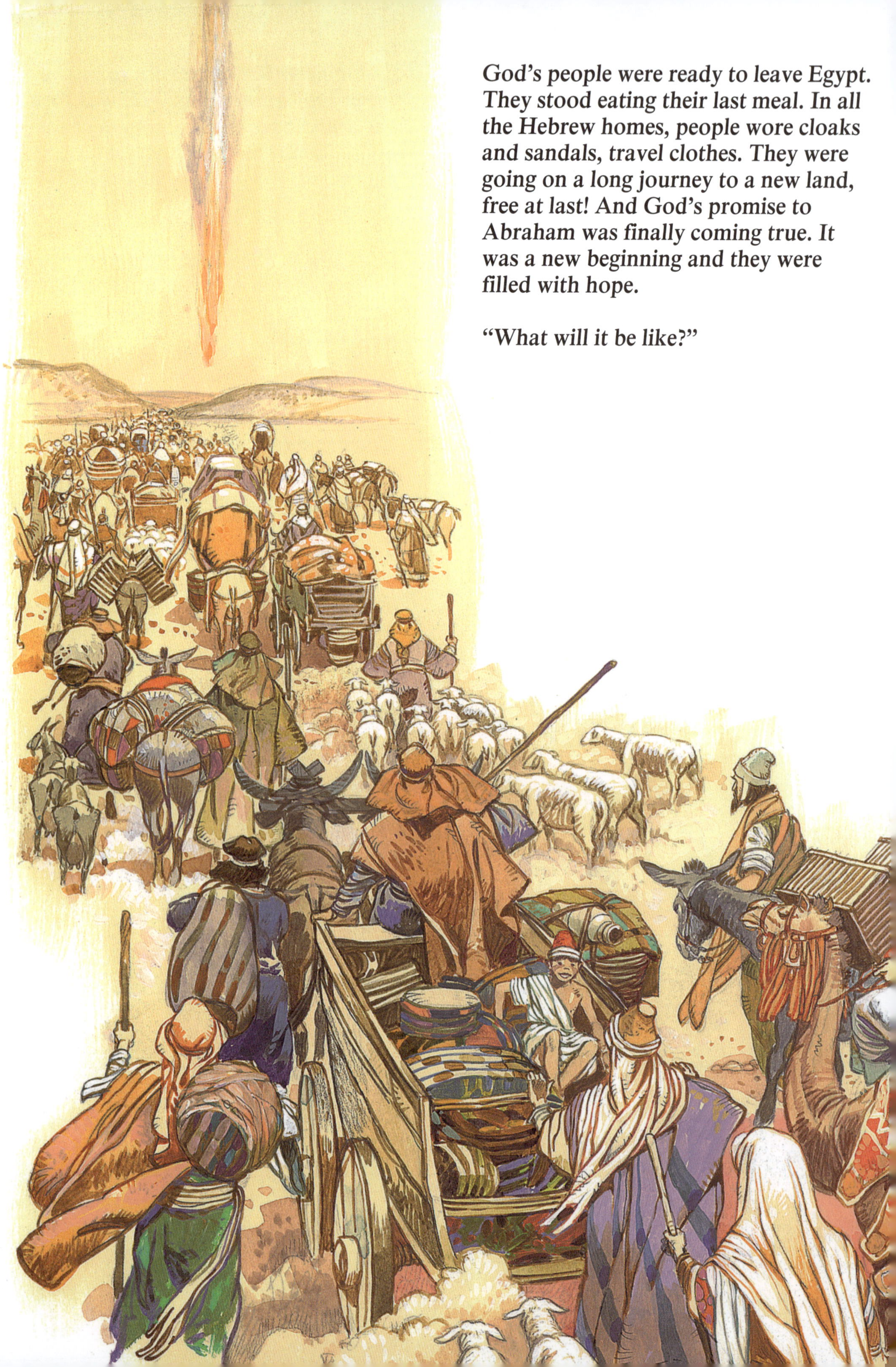

God's people were ready to leave Egypt. They stood eating their last meal. In all the Hebrew homes, people wore cloaks and sandals, travel clothes. They were going on a long journey to a new land, free at last! And God's promise to Abraham was finally coming true. It was a new beginning and they were filled with hope.

"What will it be like?"

"How far will we have to walk?" All night long the Israelites asked Moses questions.

Moses looked around "How has it happened," he asked himself. "I always thought I was a coward, and now I'm leading all these people away from the great and mighty pharaoh." All the hundreds and thousands of people had packed their things and were waiting for Moses to give the word. Would Pharaoh finally let them go?

Halfway through the mght, Moses and his people heard a strange sound. Everyone stopped talking and listened. Crying. They heard the sounds of people weeping.

"It's time!" Moses told them The word spread. A knock on the door, the shout, that was the signal. It was time to go! Pharaoh had finally given the word. They were free!

The Israelites clashed outside. Then they knew, the crying was coming from the Egyptian homes. They had all lost their eldest sons. Even Pharaoh had found his son dead. And now a terrible grief shook the land.

But the Israelites had been spared because they had done what God told them during Passover. They were God's people. If Pharaoh had believed in God, his people would have been spared too. But he chose not to believe. Now Pharaoh's heart was broken.

"Tell them to leave! Out of Egypt! I want those Hebrews gone and out of my sight!" Pharaoh sobbed.

The Israelites left Egypt as fast as they could. They took their sheep and cattle, some clothes and a little food. Moses led the way. During the day he followed a tall, thin cloud. At night the cloud became a pillar of fire, reaching down from heaven This was God's way of guiding Moses and the people.

Day and night, day and night, Moses led God's people through the desert They were afraid Pharaoh might change his mind.

One evening the Israelites thought they could feel the pounding of hoofbeats in the sand. "We're imagining things!" they laughed at each other. They had just arrived at the sea and were setting up camp.

A little boy knelt down He put his ear to the sand. "It's thumping!" The whole camp looked back the way they had just come.

Their hearts stopped.

"Pharaoh! He's coming after us!"

"Look at his army! The chariots!"

"Oh, we should have stayed in Egypt!"

"Where can we go? We're trapped by the sea!"

Moses did not have time to feel scared. He tried to calm the people, but they started running around and screaming. He said, "God, has told me He will fight for you. He says this is the last time you will ever see these Egyptians."

Then Moses stretched out his staff over the sea. The people heard a great roar as the sea split in two! Straight down the middle of the sea rose a dry path.

"Go!" Moses ordered the people. "You're not trapped anymore. God has shown us a way out Now hurry"

All night long the Israelites crossed the sea. Every single one arrived safely on the other side All their sheep and cattle made it across, as well.

In the morning, the Egyptians reached the water, just as the last Israelite scrambled up onto the other side. "If they can cross the sea, so can we" Pharaoh ordered. The chariots plunged onto the dry path through the sea.

The Israelites looked at Moses. "Now what do we do?"

Just as all the Egyptians were between the waves, Moses reached out toward the sea again. Another terrible roar shook the ground!

Moses stretched his staff over the water. The waves on both sides of the Egyptian army crashed down on top of them! God swept them away, covering them with water! Pharaoh and his men disappeared into the depths!

The people had never seen anything like it before. They cheered Moses. They cheered God. "There is no God like ours! Oh let's thank Him for saving us!" they cried. It was their first party as a free people. How they celebrated!

Moses clapped his hands and danced with the others. "Lord," he prayed, ou were right. You did stay by my side. I did not think I could lead the people and escape Egypt. But You made it happen. Thank You!" More than anything else, Moses hoped that the Israelites would never forget how much God had shown His love for them.

Now all the years Moses had spent in the desert proved useful. He knew how to find food and water in the desert. He knew how to sleep during the hot days and travel during the cool nights.

The people did not, though. And they did not like learning how. Soon after they left the sea, the people started grumbling about the heat, the food, the dryness. "We were better off as slaves in Egypt" they shouted at Moses.

Moses was their leader. He knew God loved them. "Trust God, hasn't He always taken care of us? He's promised to take us to a new land, a better land . . ." Moses knew God had not left them to die in the desert.

But no one wanted to listen. God made manna, or flakes of light bread to fall from the sky. This way the people would not go hungry. Every morning God rained down manna so the children could help their parents gather it into baskets. The people still grumbled.

Moses finally told the people they could rest and make camp. The place was at the bottom of a mountain called Sinai. God had told Moses to climb the mountain He had a special gift for Moses and the Israelite people.

Moses was away from the people forty days. All that time he talked with God on the mountaintop Moses had changed. He did not argue with God anymore. After all he had seen, Moses knew the Lord was very mighty and powerful.

The special gift which God gave Moses were two stone tablets. God had written on these rocks with His own finger He had written rules which would help His people know the difference between right and wrong These were the Ten Commandments.

The Ten Commandments were the most important gift God had ever given His people. Moses held the slabs of rock in his hands. He shook with excitement.

But then suddenly God said, "Go down at once! Your people have made a golden calf for themselves. They are calling it god They say the calf brought them out of Egypt. Got I will let My anger burn against them and they will be destroyed!" Smoke poured off the mountain.

Moses begged the Lord not to punish the people. "They are like children, Lord Did You bring them out of Egypt just to have them killed in the desert?"

All this time, Moses was swallowed up in a fire on top of the mountain This fire was just like the one in the burning bush. Its flames did not burn.

Now it was Moses who stood in the middle of the fire He was with God, as God had been with him Moses could feel the heat of God's anger. He waited for an answer.

Finally the Lord said yes to Moses. He would give the Israelites another chance. God had mercy on His people.

Moses thanked God. Then he stepped out of the fire He was the leader of the people. He would have to teach them what they had done wrong. Moses hurried down the mountain. He carried the tablets of stone carefully all the way to the camp. When he saw the people dancing around their golden calf, though, he stopped, too shocked to move.

Moses could not believe that the people would be so .. so blind, Didn't they remember what God had done to the Egyptians? Hadn't they eaten the food He gave them in the desert? Moses looked at the Ten Commandments in his hands. The very first rule told the people not to make any statues or other things and treat them like gods. Moses groaned, "They have already broken the first rule before they even had a chance to hear it."

Moses was furious! He roared, "Stop! You have done the very worst thing you could have done! You have turned away from God!

And for what? A calf of gold!"
With that, Moses raised the tablets over his head and hurled them to the ground. They shattered into a hundred pieces! The rocks, covered with God's own writing, lay broken at the foot of the mountain.

Moses punished the people. The next day he said, "I'm going back up the mountain now. I must talk to the Lord. You have done a terrible thing!"

When Moses was with God again, he said, "Please forgive them, Lord." Moses stayed another forty days on top of Mount Sinai. When the time was up, God told Moses he would let the people start over. He was very disappointed in them, though. The Lord gave Moses another set of stone tablets.

Moses brought these down to the people and read the rules to them. The people promised to try and be good. They listened to the rules and nodded their heads. "Yes," some said. "They make good sense."

Then the people moved on through the desert. They followed wherever Moses led them No matter how far they went, though, they would never forget the look on Moses' face when he came down from that mountain. His face had shone like the sun!

Moses' face had shone because, dunng his second time on the mountaintop, Moses saw God He was the only man to see God face to face The Lord walked right by Moses He stood with him, just as any man would with his friend Moses became God's friend. Seeing God had lit up Moses' face!

This was not the only time Moses' face shone from the glory of God. Wherever Moses told the people to camp, he always put up one special tent for the Lord In that tent Aaron and his sons carefully placed the Ten Commandments.

Moses visited the tent often. He went there to talk with God He always came out of the tent with his face glowing. This was a sign to the people that their Moses was not just any leader. Moses was God's chosen leader.

Even though the people had promised to be good, it did not take them long to start grumbling and complaining again.

"It's too hoe"

"We should never have left Egypt!" When they did not have enough to eat, they moaned. When they did have enough to eat, they groaned.

"Where is God anyway?" They were not at all thankful for the food and water God gave them every day.

Moses tried his best to teach the people. That is what leaders are for. "Just think of where we are going. God promised to take us safely to a new land, the promised land! Trust Him, He has never forgotten you!"

But the people chose not to listen. Even when they had camped at a place very near to the promised land, the people grumbled. "We've seen that land. It's full of enemy tribes!"

"We don't want to live there!" The people shouted at Moses.

"You know what we think? There is no God!" They had completely forgotten the power of God. They had forgotten that they had ever been slaves in Egypt. They had forgotten about Mount Sinai. They stopped following Moses and listening to him. Now there was no way God could reach them with His love.

There was nothing Moses could do. No one would listen to him! Finally God grew so angry at the people that He said they would have to spend forty years wandering through the desert until they arrived at their new homes.

Wandering for forty years meant that all the people who had grumbled would die of old age before they reached the promised land.

The Lord would start over with the children of those He had brought out of Egypt, the children of the grumblers In forty years those children would be grown. By then God's people would finally be ready to trust Him.

Moses groaned inside when he heard the news. He had never wanted the job of leading such a stubborn people. Yet now he had forty more years to go before he finished the job.

During that time he would often sigh, "I don't know if I can do this." Moses felt weak when the people kept making the same mistakes over and over again. He often thought about giving up and saying, "It's no use."

Each time Moses came to God's tent and prayed about his doubts, God said, "Moses, I am with you. I have chosen you." This helped lift Moses' worries. It was enough for Moses that God was on his side.

For forty long years Moses led God's people around, through, in and out of the desert. A trip which was only about one hundred miles should have only lasted a few weeks. Instead it dragged on for forty years! Throughout it all, there was never one day when Moses stopped hying to be the best leader possible. He was not bossy, but caring, like a shepherd for his sheep.

At the end of that time, all the people who had said they didn't believe in God were dead of old age. Their children were grown, and had children of their own. These people believed in God, even though they had not seen what God had done for them in Egypt. They trusted Him and looked forward to seeing the promised land.

One day, God told Moses to hand the job of leader over to someone else. Moses was a hundred and twenty years old. He was the only old person left. Even Aaron was dead by then.

He called all the people together. "Remember to follow the Law. Listen to your new leader. And never make the same mistakes your parents made. Believe in God and He will always be by your side."

Moses knew what he was talking about. He had started out being the most unsure of men. No matter what, God had always shown him what to do and made everything come out all right. Moses did not take the credit, he gave it all to God.

The time had come for Moses to leave the earth and be with the Lord All alone he climbed to the top of a mountain There stretched out before him was . the promised lands "I can see it all!" Moses cried. He had led the people so long and so far This was what he had waited all his life to see.

God had said Moses could look at the land, but he would never actually enter the land. This time Moses did not argue with God He said yes. After all, Moses was the friend of God. And that made everything worth it.

While standing on that mountain, Moses died. God came and buried Moses' body Himself. Moses was one of the most important men to ever mold the history of God's people. For forty years Moses was a prince. For forty years he thought of himself as a nobody. And for forty years Moses was God's choice to lead His people to the promised land.

You can find the story of Moses in the Old Testament
in the book of Exodus, Numbers and Deuteronomy.

MIRIAM

God's Chosen Leader

By Marlee Alex

Illustrated by Florence Magnin

MIRIAM

A Woman Who Saw the Answer to Her Prayers

By Marlee Alex

Illustrated by Florence Magnin

Throw every baby boy into the Nile River," Pharaoh ordered. "Let the crocodiles have them or let them drown!"

Pharaoh was a powerful and cruel king. He was cruel because he was terribly afraid Although he had made the Hebrew people living in Egypt his slaves, over the years they had become too plentiful. They kept having large families and were becoming a strong people. And Pharaoh was afraid someday they might become too powerful to control.

Hebrew mothers shrieked as their baby boys were torn from their arms. The king's soldiers showed no mercy. But one mother whispered to her oldest child, "Miriam, my dear daughter, help me braid these reeds. We are going to make a basket sealed with tar that will float. Your baby brother will just fit inside it. We'll hide the basket among the reeds in the over."

Miriam began to cry. "Mother, how can we set him out on the river? He will drift with the current and be lost. Why, he's just grown big enough to smile at me!" Teardrops splashed down on Miriam's bare feet.

"We must be brave," replied her mother. "This way your brother has a chance to survive. Perhaps the God of our fathers will make a way to spare his life."

Some of Miriam's friends had seen their baby brothers carried away to be killed Miriam knew her mother was right. "But Mother," she said, drying her eyes, "at least let me watch over the basket from the shore. Then maybe I can see what happens to him. I won't let anyone see me. I promise."

Miriam's mother wrinkled her brow and sighed as Miriam pleaded, "Please mother, please!"

"All right," conceded her mother. "But stay well hidden."

Miriam bent down and lifted her little brother from his mother's breast. He was full and sleepy. She nestled him under the soft blankets in the basket, but her hands were trembling. Looking into the watery eyes of her mother, she said, "Don't be sad I'm helping. I'll do my best."

Together Miriam and her mother covered the basket and started of toward the river. Along the street they passed a small company of the king's soldiers, marching from house to house. Miriam heard one of the soldiers say, "There was another infant born to a family around here somewhere." Then he stopped Miriam's mother, "Hey woman, tell us! Who has a new baby in this neighborhood? The king's orders are to kill every baby boy."

For a moment Miriam's mother was speechless. But Miriam chirped, "Come, let's get this basketful of dirty clothes washed." She pulled on her mother's skirts.

Then Miriam's mother got an idea. She did not want to lie to the soldiers. But she had to protect the life of her child asleep in the basket. "I hope to hear soon that the baby has been delivered," she replied. And in one way she was right, for she was hoping God would deliver her baby boy from death.

The soldiers grumbled, "We'll be back next week," as they marched off again.

At the river's edge Miriam pulled the basket cradling her baby brother into the thick bulrushes. "Lord, protect my baby brother," she prayed. "Let him live. Let him grow up."

Miriam's mother pulled leaves and branches around the basket and turned back toward home. Her body shivered, but not from the cold. Miriam stayed hidden, pretending to wade in the shallow water. She pushed her bare toes into the wet sand along the shore. "Let him live. Let him live," she prayed.

The small braided basket was rocked by the gentle river current Gradually it rocked loose of the reeds and rushes where it had been placed. It began to drift slowly downstream. Miriam followed from the shore, stopping whenever the basket became lodged among the reeds. She wondered, "What shall I do when the basket floats so far away I can no longer follow?"

But Miriam's worries were suddenly interrupted by the giggling and chatter of girls not much older than herself They were running toward the river. "Ohhh!" gasped Miriam out loud. "The princess!" Miriam could see by the girl's pretty dress that this was the king's daughter. The princess and her handmaidens were coming to bathe at the river. Miriam was afraid she had been discovered by them. Splashing in the water, she hoped the princess would believe she was only playing. "If only they do not notice the basket nearby," she thought.

But the noise had awakened Miriam's baby brother. "Waaa, waaaaa," he cried. The princess immediately saw the little reed basket, half-hidden by river foliage. "Look! Someone has hidden a baby here in the river!" she exclaimed. "This must be one of the Hebrew babies!"

"Isn't he sweet?" cried one of her servants as she dragged the basket to the shore. "The poor little fellow is hungry."

Miriam's heart beat wildly. Her mind was racing. What if the princess took the baby to her father, the cruel king?

Miriam pretended to act as surprised as the other girls at the discovery of the baby. She stepped forward. "If the baby is hungry, I know a mother who can give milk," she told them. "Shall I go and fetch her for you?"

"Why, yes!" exclaimed the princess. "Run along and get her. I will pay her to feed and care for this baby until he is old enough to live with me at the palace. I will raise him as my own son and my father will not hurt him." The princess cuddled the baby in her arms. "His name will be Moses, because I drew him out of the water," she said.

Miriam ran back to her mother as fast as the wind. "He did it!" she shouted. "The Lord has answered our prayers!" That day Miriam's mother was given back her own baby to love and care for until he was old enough to walk, talk, and eat by himself.

Many years passed. Miriam grew up. And so did her little brother. But for most of his life Moses had lived like a prince in the beautiful palace, while Miriam and her parents had been slaves of the cruel king.

The king made all the Hebrews' lives miserable. He forced them to work for him all day in the hot sun. They carried heavy loads of grain from the fields and made endless piles of bricks out of straw and mud. Each year the king gave them more back-breaking jobs. He forced them to build great cities and monuments in Egypt.

Miriam spent most of her days in huge vats, tramping water clay and straw with her bare feet. Beads of sweat formed on her face and ran down her neck. Sometimes she paused and looked toward the distant palace where her younger brother lived. Once she even caught a glimpse of him, now a strong young man, walking on the balcony. His jeweled rings and golden arm bands gleamed in the sunlight.

Miriam looked down at her own tattered clothes and thin form. "Dear Lord," she cried out loud, "our people are wasting away in this hot, cruel land. Even our young people grow thinner and weaker day by day. Listen to our groans!"

"Hey, you! Slave!" snarled one of the Egyptian slave drivers. "Keep moving!" His whip cracked through the air and stung Miriam's arm. "Double time!" he barked.

Miriam bit her tongue to keep from yelping. She choked on her own tears. She had seen other slaves whipped to death for complaining. Miriam kept her eyes on the Egyptian palace and began to tramp the clay even harder. "Moses is in there somewhere," she remembered. And that thought brought her comfort. "God, help us, all of us," she prayed silently. Then her eyes searched the palace for yet another glimpse of gold gleaming in the sunlight.

One day Miriam and her family heard some terrible news Several neighbors were standing outside talking. "The princess's son has killed an Egyptian slave driver!" one said.

"Yes," another answered. "He hid the dead body in the sand, thinking no one would find out!"

"But haven't you heard?" questioned a third neighbor. "Moses has already fled from Egypt. He left the palace in quite a hurry. He must be so scared."

Miriam was paralyzed with shock. "Moses has left Egypt? What will become of him?" she wondered. "And what will become of the rest of us?"

Miriam tried to remember the stories her father had told her as a child. She knew that long ago Abraham, Isaac, and Jacob had been promised a land flowing with milk and honey. God had promised to give this rich land to their children's children, the Hebrew people.

Miriam called upon the Lord again, "Where is this land? When will your promise be fulfilled? How can our people be set free?"

As the hard years slowly rolled by, God seemed deaf to Miriam's cries. But she kept praying. And as she did, her faith in God's promise became strong and sure. The Egyptian palace looked empty and cold without Moses, but the promised land of her dreams grew more dear and more clear. Miriam spoke to her people, the Hebrew slaves, about this promise. She encouraged them to believe, although the fulfillment seemed impossible. She became a prophetess for her people.

One extraordinary day, Moses showed up again at the doorstep of the Egyptian palace. His face was sunburned and wrinkled. His hands were scratched by the thorny bushes of the desert. "Pharaoh," he declared, "the Lord says you must let my people go!"

Pharaoh did not know who this man was. "Who are you and who is the Lord?" he laughed. "You are wasting my time. Go away!"

The news of Moses' return spread quickly among the slaves. When Miriam heard of it she jumped for joy. "Surely this is God's work," she told the others.

But most of the Hebrew slaves were not impressed. "Who does Moses think he is?" they asked. "Does he want to rule over us now himself?"

When the Egyptian slave masters heard of Moses' demand they began to treat the Hebrews even more brutally than before. "You lazy fools," they shouted. "From now on you don't get any more straw to make bricks with. Find straw yourselves if you can! But keep making just as many bricks as before." The whips of the slave masters ripped the shirts off the backs of any who grumbled.

Miriam went out into the hay fields to search for stubble which she could mix with her vat of clay. Late that night she was still working, trying to finish making her daily quota of bricks. The next day when the bricks had dried, they crumbled and broke, for there had not been enough straw to make the clay strong. Miriam's dreams for a better life seemed to be crumbling just like her bricks.

Moses stayed in Egypt, however, insisting that Pharaoh let the Hebrews go. God struck Egypt with one terrible plague after another. Yet Pharaoh continued to refuse the Hebrews their freedom because he wanted all the slaves he could get.

Then Moses told his own people, 'Tonight the shadow of death will pass over Egypt and strike down the firstborn of every Egyptian family. But you are to slaughter a lamb at twilight and with its blood paint the doors of your homes. When the Lord sees the blood, He will pass over you, and death shall not touch those who sleep within."

Miriam and her family carefully poured the blood of a lamb into a basin. They dipped a branch of hyssop into it and smeared the blood onto the doorjamb of their hut. Then they put on their cloaks, tied up their sandals, and waited for the shadow of death to pass by their home.

At midnight the air seemed suddenly cold and clamp Miriam shuddered as the sound of loud weeping and wailing came from the windows of Egyptian neighbors. By the very early hours of the morning there was not one Egyptian family who had not lost a child. Even Pharaoh's oldest son died that night. But the Hebrew children slept unharmed, and among them not a dog barked.

While it was still dark Pharaoh stumbled out onto his balcony and shouted, “Get out, you Hebrews! All of you! Take your little ones and your old ones, your sons and your daughters, your flocks and your herds. Don’t let me see a single one of you ever again!” Pharaoh turned back inside the palace, bitterly weeping over the loss of his boy.

As the first rays of dawn pierced the blackness of night, a white pillar of cloud rose from the ground and into the sky. Miriam rubbed her eyes and stared. "Do you see it?" she called to her neighbors. "Do you recognize God in the cloud? He never forgot us. He has come to deliver us from slavery after all!"

Miriam left her home and was hurrying down the street when an Egyptian woman appeared in a doorway. She was the wife of a slave master. The woman threw a heap of golden jewelry at Miriam's feet. 'Take this and get out!" she sobbed. "My son is dead. What good is this gold to me now?"

Miriam scooped up the jewelry from the dusty street and hurried on, thmking, "Why, this gold does not sparkle as I thought it did But we're finally on our way!"

The pillar of cloud now began to move before the huge crowd of Hebrew men, women, children, and animals. God led them through the narrow streets of towns and villages. Then, instead of heading up over the hills, the pillar of cloud moved out into what seemed an endless stretch of hot desert sand.

The gritty sand filled their sandals and lodged between their toes. It was whipped by breezes through their clothes. It stuck in the corners of their eyes. Nor could they keep it out of their food and water. The children cried and complained. "When will we reach the beautiful land?" they asked over and over again. "When will we be across this desert?"

Miriam patted the children's small heads. "Keep your courage up," she said as they tramped onward. She started to hum a familiar tune for them.

But the grownups interrupted, "We are going the wrong way. There is nothing ahead but the sea, and we have no boats with which to cross it."

Then a little girl shouted, "Listen! Don't you hear something?"

"Look! Behind us!" shouted her father. "It's Pharaoh and his horse-drawn chariots!"

The Hebrew crowd panicked. Pharaoh was riding toward them at a furious rate. He had decided not to let them go after all.

The Hebrews cried out to Moses, who was walking out in front of them. "Why did you bring us out here to be pinned down by Pharaoh, trapped between the desert and the sea? We should never have left Egypt!"

Miriam looked into the angry, frightened faces of those she had labored alongside as makers of Egyptian bricks and builders of Egyptian towers. Her eyes met those of a terrified young woman with a baby tied to her back and two other children clinging to her legs. Miriam was wondering, "Can they be right? Are we to die out here?" But Miriam could not forget how God had answered her childhood prayers for Moses and had returned Moses to them two times, once as a baby and once as a leader. "No," she told the young woman, "God has brought us out of Egypt, and He will bring us into a land where there is a bright future for your children."

Moses' voice quieted the entire crowd "The Lord will fight for you today" he declared.

As Moses spoke, the pillar of cloud moved behind the people, casting a dark shadow over the approaching Egyptian horsemen. Moses stretched his arm out toward the sea lying before them.

"Come," cried Miriam. "Run! March! Let's go!" The people hurried ahead and stepped into the waves lapping at the seashore. The waves split apart and banked, leaving a dry path across the floor of the sea. All that night the Hebrews fled between the walls of water, across the sea, and onto dry land.

Finally, the last family reached safety. But Pharaoh's chariots were still chasing them. This time Moses stretched his arm out over the sea from the other shoreline, and as he did so the walls of water caved in. The Egyptian soldiers, horses, and chariots were swept away and drowned.

The Hebrews watched what happened as if in a dream. But Miriam dug into her traveling gear and pulled out a tambourine. She raised it into the air with a shimmy. She dashed it against the palm of her other

hand. She began to sway, light as a bubble. In and out among the people she danced as the jingling of the tambourine rang over the sea. Then she began to sing, "Sing to the Lord, for He is great! Sing to the Lord, for He is great!"

The young woman with the baby on her back raised her hands in the air and began to clap to the rhythm. The two children pranced around her feet. Another woman grabbed a tambourine and followed Miriam through the crowd. One by one little girls, weary mothers, and stoop-shouldered old women joined the circle of jubilant dancers, as the men stood nearby and clapped. They all sang the song of Miriam. "Sing to the Lord, for He is great. He has

hurled horses and riders into the sea!" The early-morning, desert air was filled with music.

The Hebrews were on their way to the Promised Land.

As a child Miriam learned to trust God and to pray. She saw how God answered her prayers for her baby brother, Moses When she grew up she became a prophetess. She told people about God's ways and encouraged them to believe in Him even when it seemed impossible.

But Miriam was not perfect. Once, during the long journey to the Promised Land, she criticized her brother Moses because she was jealous of him. "Does the Lord speak only through Moses?" she asked. "Doesn't He also speak through me?" The Lord became angry with Minam, but forgave her when Moses offered up prayers for her.

Miriam will be remembered as an energetic, hardworking woman who trusted the Lord when times were hard and kept faith through many difficult years. Miriam was a woman who saw the answers to her prayers.

You can find the story of Miriam in the Old Testament
in the book of Exodus, chapters 2:1-10 and 15:20-21.

DEBORAH

A Woman Who Brought an Entire Nation Back to God

By Marlee Alex

Illustrated by José Pérez Montero

DEBORAH

A Woman Who Brought an Entire Nation Back to God

By Marlee Alex

Illustrated by José Pérez Montero

N of a cloud was in sight as little Deborah peered out of the goat-skin tent. The sun poured diamond beams from the sky over the rocky cliff and spilled them onto the sand before her. Heat waves shimmered across the horizon. The girl's small hands fumbled for her head covering and pulled it over her face. Nearly hiding her eyes, the billowy, white fabric protected her from the glare of the light. She flapped the tent door behind her and moved quickly toward the shade of the giant palm tree nearby.

Desert winds blew softly. Grains of sand swirled around Deborah's bare feet as she ran. "Goodbye!" she waved to her father and brothers. They were headed for school in the neighboring village where Deborah's father was a teacher.

Under the wide branches of the palm tree Deborah found refuge from the heat and began to gather the sweet-tasting palm dates lying on the ground around her. The huge, prickly trunk of this tree had often been her backrest on cool evenings. For as long as she could remember, her family had eaten their evening meals here and talked about the boys' days at school.

Deborah wished she could go to school. But she knew that girls in Israel, the country where she lived, had to stay home and help with household chores. In the evenings, Deborah often asked her father many questions. She wondered about the God of her father, whose name was Jehovah. No one dared say this name out loud. Jehovah was a powerful and mysterious God. "But He loves His people, the children of Israel," Deborah's father had told her.

"I want to know this God myself," Deborah

O often thought. ne evenmg, Deborah was playing hide-and-seek with her brothers among the neighbors' tents. Hiding behind a loose tent flap, she heard a grown-up say, "King Jabrn's army passed close to here yesterday."

Another neighbor answered, "Next time it will be our tents they tear down, our women they carry off!" Deborah shuddered. But she soon forgot about it and scampered away to find a better hiding place.

As Deborah grew older, the iron chariots of King Jabin's army often rumbled within hearing distance of where she lived. The camel caravans of merchants and traders were seen less and less often. For the people of Israel, any kind of travel was dangerous. They risked their lives even when visiting the wells in the countryside. Enemy soldiers hid in the hills with bows and arrows, waiting to attack those who came to draw water.

With each passing year, the village of tents where Deborah lived dwindled. Many of the tent dwellers pulled up stakes and moved to the cities "We are tired of being afraid," they told those who stayed behind. "The stone walls of the city will keep us safe."

Deborah heard the villagers complaining as they packed their things. "The gods are deaf. They accept neither our sacrifices nor our prayers."

"Still, we may be no safer in the city," they admitted. "King Jabin's army threatens it at his slightest whim. City people are just as afraid as we are."

"That's right, we are never safe, not even in our own country. King Jabin and the heathen Canaanites are pressing in on us from all sides, making life miserable."

Deborah did not understand everything the villagers said. She did not understand why they reacted to the Canaanites in fear rather than by trusting in God. "Why don't they call on the Lord God?" she asked her father. "Why don't they seek Him, the only One who can help?"

Deborah's father was silent for a long, long time. "They have turned from Him," he answered at last. "They have forgotten His name. In the days of peace, they grew tired of Him and discarded Him like an old coat. They chose new, heathen gods. Now that there is trouble, they are ashamed to call on Him again."

"Then, is there no hope for Israel?" asked Deborah.

"There is always hope, Deborah," her father replied. "We must ask God to make us wise and give us a brave leader."

Deborah kept asking questions as she grew up. Her questions were sometimes difficult to answer. Her father taught her from the holy Scriptures and repeated the stories that he had heard from his father.

There came a day when Deborah's father noticed Deborah actually beginning to answer her own questions She seemed to have wisdom concerning things even he had wondered about. Deborah began talking to the people in the tent village around her, challenging them to trust in the one true God.

P. Montero

"How can she be so confident?" the villagers asked one another. "Where does she get such courage?"

Before long, people in other villages of Israel heard about this young woman named Deborah, who lived near the great palm tree between Ramah and Bethel. They wanted to listen to her. Some of these people had seen loved ones hurt by King Jabin's soldiers. Others were tense and angry, for the Canaanites living in the hill country threatened them constantly.

Deborah offered comfort to those who came to her. From the Scriptures she gave them a reason to hope. Deborah believed in the future and in the chance for a better life. But she warned her people to repent and turn from worshipping false gods. She told them that Jehovah, the God of Israel, wanted all their love and trust.

Before long, people began coming to Deborah with their personal quarrels. They believed she could settle their arguments for them. Deborah was wise and patient. She knew the right questions to ask in order to find out who was right and who was wrong. And she never stopped challenging the Israelites to be brave, to destroy their idols, and to pray for deliverance from Canaanite kings like King Jabin.

King Jabin wanted to destroy the government of the Israelites. He routinely ordered his soldiers to ride through their city gates and frighten the judges holding court there. But Jabin never attacked the village court of Deborah. "She is only a woman," he told his general. "She can't possibly cause any trouble. Don't bother with her." But King Jabin was wrong.

Deborah was to become one of the greatest judges Israel had ever had. The place where she held court became famous, known as the Palm of Deborah.

"Lord God of Israel," Deborah prayed at the start of every day, "You know I shall be busy today. I want to speak Your truth. Give me Your wisdom." God gave Deborah His own messages to pass onto the people.

One day, Deborah sent a message to an Israelite named Barak. Barak lived in Naphtali, a neighboring area of the country. When he arrived at Deborah's palm tree, Deborah told him, "The Lord God of Israel has appointed you to raise an army of ten thousand men. He wants you to lead them in an attack against the armies of King Jabin. You are to assemble your troops on the top of Mount Tabor The Lord Himself will draw Jabin's army to the Kishon River below, led by mighty General Sisera. They will have nine hundred chariots with them But you and your foot soldiers will win the battle!"

Barak turned pale. He stared at Deborah in astonishment. Barak was brave, but not that brave. He knew very well he needed God's help in every battle. And he knew Deborah was led and directed by God He swallowed the lump in his throat, then answered, "If you will go with me, Deborah, I will go But if you don't march alongside the rest of us, then I'm going to stay home."

"All right," Deborah smiled. "I'll start preparing right away. But I tell you, Barak, you will not be the hero. When the battle is over, the honor of the victory will go to a woman!"

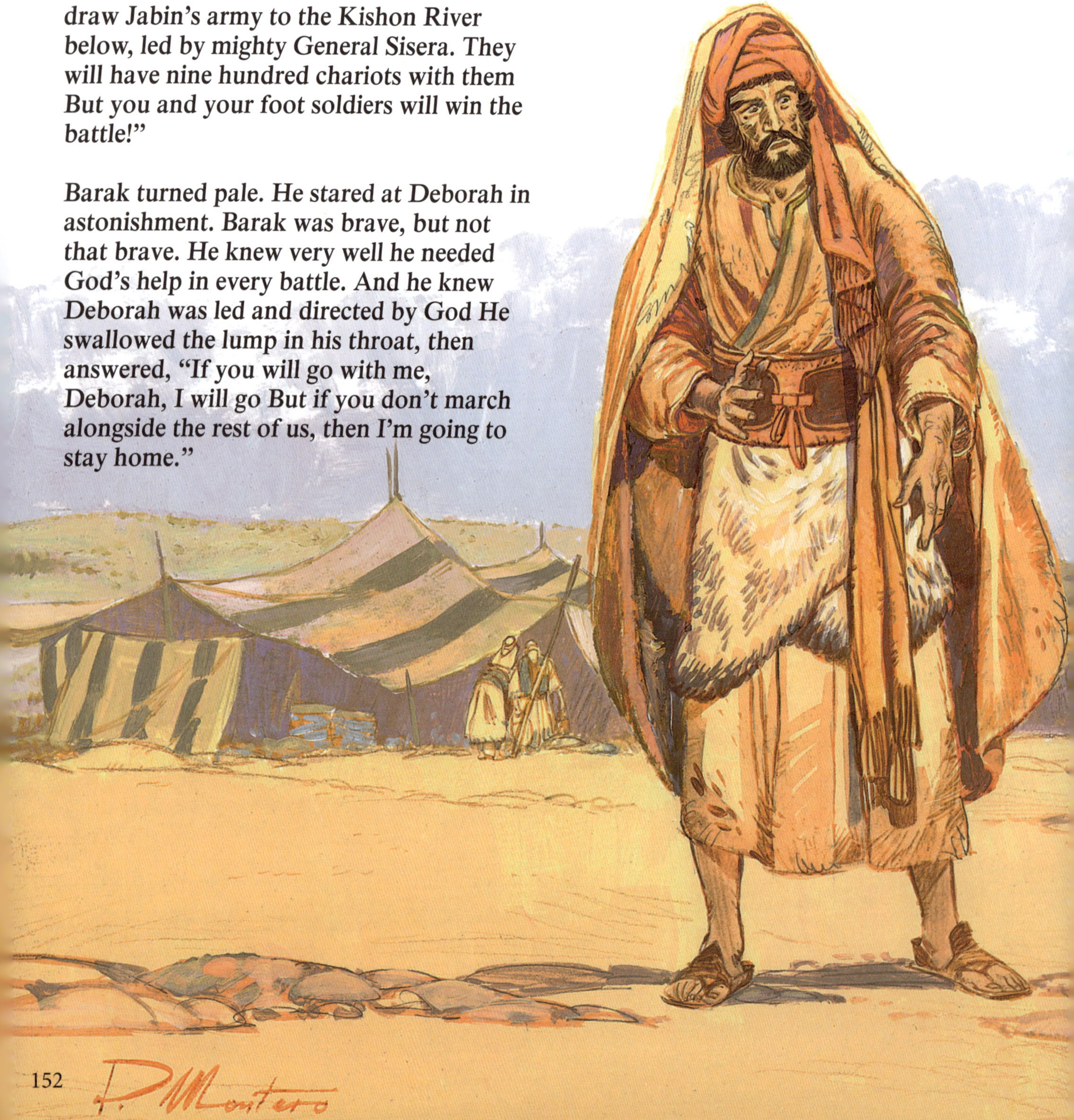

Barak thought, of course, that Deborah meant the honor would be hers. He was more than willing to let her be the heroine. He left Deborah's palm and hiked back to Naphtali, where he began to organize an army. Ten thousand men bravely volunteered Deborah soon joined the men and led them to the top of Mount Tabor.

Word came to General Sisera, leader of King Jabin's army, that a company of foot soldiers was camped at Mount Tabor, intending to provoke a battle. "Ha, ha, ha," laughed General Sisera.

"Those fools! They want a battle, do they? Then we will give it to them. Ha, ha, ha! What a battle we will give to them, Servant, sharpen my sword and get the horses ready. We will tear the very feet off those pitiful footmen who think they are so brave!"

King Jabin's army was feared most of all for its terrible iron chariots. Sharp scythes were fastened to the wheels of each chariot. When the chariots were driven into an army of footmen, the scythes could cut quickly through bone and muscle, destroying any enemy. And General Sisera was determined to make full use of the chariots' power.

General Sisera's soldiers rode to the foot of Mown Tabor, close to the Kishon River. The Kishon was really just a narrow stream that trickled toward the valley. Sisera's men could easily drive the horse chariots through it from one bank to the other. As the enemy assembled below, Deborah spoke to Barak on the peak of Mount Tabor. "Have courage!" she exclaimed. "This is the day of victory over General Sisera The Lord goes before you. He has prepared the victory. It is time to defeat the enemy!"

Just before daylight Barak and Deborah led their men down the slopes of the mountain Closer and closer they came to the heavily armed soldiers of King Jabin. Barak's men knew their only advantage was that God stood on their side. Their weapons could never penetrate the armor of the king's soldiers, nor had they any defense against the plunging chariots. They would not even be able to take the enemy by surprise. But Barak's men were ready to do the nght thing. Deborah was praying fervently.

Suddenly, it seemed the stars began to fall from the sky, plummeting down like balls of ice and fire. General Sisera's soldiers were thrown into a panic. Their horses stampeded and ran off in all directions General Sisera jumped from his chariot and fled into the hills as fast as his feet could carry him. The Kishon River swelled, overflowed its banks, and swallowed up those Canaanite soldiers too slow to get away.

Barak's men chased the soldiers who were running into the hills and caught up with them, tool They fought until the last enemy was dead. Only General Sisera managed to get away.

Escaping through the underbrush, Sisera passed the tent of a woman whose husband was friends with King Jabin. The woman's name was Jael.

Jael shouted to Sisera as he ran by, "Slow down, Come into my tent and hide until the Israelites have passed by. I'll give you a cold drink and a place to rest until they are gone!"

Sisera was hot, sweaty, and exhausted. "Oh, thank you," he panted. "I accept your kindness gladly." Then he hurried into her tent Jael took her finest serving bowl and gave sera a refreshing drink. She showed him a place on the floor where he could hide and covered him with a blanket. Before long, Sisera fell fast asleep. But Sisera did not know that at that very moment he was in far greater danger than he had been on the battlefield.

Jael was a strong woman who earned her livelihood making sturdy goatskin tents. And she did not take kindly to the cruel soldiers of King Jabin Once Sisera began snoring in peaceful sleep, Jael grabbed an iron tent peg and placed the tip of it in front of his ear. With a mighty swing of her hammer she pounded the peg through his head and into the ground. Sisera died instantly. The fame of Jael spread throughout Israel. She became a heroine that day, and the honor of the final victory was gained by a woman, just as Deborah had prophesied.

When the battle of the day was over Deborah wrote a song of praise to God while the impressions of His mercy were fresh on her mind and heart. Deborah put the story of what had happened that day to music so fathers and mothers could sing it to their children and their children's children for years to come. "The Lord is mighty, His presence is with us!" she sang out. "The young leaders of Israel are full of faith and obedient to Him! Those who love Him will shine like the rising sun!"

King Jabin's army never recovered from the defeat by Barak and the men who marched under Deborah's direction The Canaanite people and their kings became weaker and weaker. The people of Israel grew confident, brave, and strong.

Deborah continued as a judge in Israel She taught her people that God's presence is the best advantage over any enemy. "But, like Barak's soldiers, you must be determined to use that advantage and carry out bravely what God calls you to do," she often told them.

Deborah set a great example for the men and women of her country and time. And she brought an entire nation back to God.

You can find the story of Deborah in the Old Testament
in the book of Judges, chapters 4 and 5.

RUTH

A Woman Whose Loyalty Was Stronger Than Her Grief

By Marlee Alex

Illustrated by Alfonso Ruano

RUTH

A Woman Whose Loyalty Was Stronger Than Her Grief

By Marlee Alex

Illustrated by Alfonso Ruano

Once upon a time there was a young woman named Ruth who lived in the land of Moab. Ruth was married to a nice young man whose mother, Naomi, lived with them. Ruth and Naomi were good friends. Nearby lived Naomi's oldest son and his wife, Orpha. They were all one close family.

For several years life was good. Ruth had no children of her own, but she was content and happy. Yet not in her wildest dreams did she imagine she would one day be the great-grandmother of a mighty king.

Years passed Then the husbands of both Ruth and Orpha died. It was a very sad time. Ruth and Orpha missed their husbands terribly, and Naomi missed her two sons. Besides grieving for their loved ones, the women were worried about the future. In those days, a woman could not take a job and earn a living for herself. Now there was no one to take care of Ruth and Orpha and their mother-in-law, Naomi.

Naomi sat down with the two younger women. Tears filled her eyes. "Ten years ago I came from the land of Israel," she said. " I was born, raised and married there. My two sons were born there before we moved to Moab. Now that they are dead I feel homesick for my own country. So I've decided to go back to Israel where people worship the one true God. Besides, the crops have been good there this year. There will be plenty to eat. I'll get along all right."

Ruth interrupted, "But, dear Naomi, what shall we do? We love you as if you were our own mother."

Naomi answered, "You are welcome to come with me if you like. But it would be better for you to return to the homes of your parents here in Moab. They could help each of you find another husband. You should get married again, and raise families of your own. You deserve better lives than I could ever provide you."

Naomi kissed Ruth and held her tight, then she turned to Orpha and hugged her. "I love both of you as if you were my own children. You have truly been loyal daughters to me," she said tenderly. "Go on home now, for I have nothing left to give you."

Ruth was crying Then Orpha started crying. Naomi stopped trying to fight back her own tears The women thought they would never see each other again. Orpha kissed Naomi once more then packed her things and returned to the home of her childhood.

But Ruth clung to Naomi and cried, "I want to go with you to Israeli want to stay with you."

Naomi insisted, "Look Ruth, Orpha has gone back to her own people. You must do the same."

"Please don't make me go back!" Ruth pleaded. "I want to go wherever you go, and live wherever you live. I want to become one of the people of Israel, like you, and worship the one true God. When I die, I want to be buried beside you."

Ruth was not going to change her mind. So Naomi did not say another word.

The two women set off for Israel on foot. After many days and nights they finally arrived in Bethlehem, the village where Naomi had grown up. Ruth and Naomi were tired. They had no more money. They were hungry and thirsty. Their feet were blistered and sore.

Everyone in Bethlehem was very busy, for the barley harvest had just begun. But people stopped and stared, wondering who the two strangers were. Then an elderly lady recognized her old friend. "Could this possibly be Naomi?" she asked.

"You must not call me Naomi anymore," Naomi answered, "for that name means 'pleasant', My life is not pleasant anymore. Call me a name that means 'bitter' now, for that is how I feel. I left this town full and happy, but I am returning empty." Naomi was feeling sorry for herself. But Ruth determined to cheer her up.

After a good night's sleep, Ruth said to Naomi, "I'll try to get something for us to eat The barley is being harvested now. Perhaps I can gather some of the grain left over in the fields. Then we can make barley soup."

So Ruth tied a scarf on her head and left for the countryside. She asked permission to gather the leftover grain at the first field she came to, then began to work along the edges of the field. The field belonged to a man named Boaz. Ruth did not know Boaz was a relative of Naomi.

That afternoon Boaz came out to the field to inspect the harvest "Who is that girl over there?" he asked his workers.

"She's new in town," one of them answered "She is Naomi's daughter-in-law, from Moab. She was out here bright and early this morning and has hardly stopped to rest."

Boaz called to Ruth. "Hello!" he shouted. "It's quite all right You can stay in my field and take whatever grain has fallen behind the reapers Just keep behind the women.

I'll make sure none of the men bother you. And when you get thirsty, drink from the water jars my servants fill."

Ruth was amazed that Boaz was so friendly. "Why are you being so kind to a stranger like me?" she asked

'Well, I know who you are" Boaz replied. You are Naomi's daughter-in-law. I've heard about how good you have been to her. You even left your own mother and father in Moab to come to Israel and make a home under the wings of the Lord God. May God bless you and your work!"

"Oh, thank you sire" Ruth exclaimed. "And thank you for your kindness even though I haven't been hired by you."

At lunch time Boaz called out, "Come, Ruth. You can share our food." Ruth joined Boazand the other reapers. She was given all the roasted grain and bread she could eat. She wrapped some of it in her scarf to take home to Naomi.

When Ruth returned to the field after lunch, Boaz told his servants, "Let her take all the grain she wants In fact, I want you to pull up some stalks of grain and drop them on purpose for her to find."

Ruth continued working until evening, then returned to Naomi. Ruth beat the grain from the straw, and discovered there was enough barley to fill a large basket. That much barley would last a long time.

Naomi was surprised and pleased. “Where in the world did you get all this, Ruth? Someone must have been very kind to you. Bless his hearts Tell me, how did you manage to gather so much?”

Ruth told Naomi all about Boaz and what had happened that day.

“Praise the Lord!” Naomi exclaimed. “Did you know this man, Boaz, is a relative of ours?”

"No, but I wondered why he was so kind to me. He even told me I could stay and gather grain in his field until the end of harvest!"

"That's wonderful Ruth. And if you keep close to the other women reapers like Boaz said, you'll be safe. I won't have to worry about you at all."

Ruth and Naomi had plenty to eat all summer long, and began to build a new life. Then one day Naomi said to Ruth, "It is time you were getting married again, Ruth. I'd like to help you find a good man."

"Naomi, we are doing just fine. God will continue to provide for us," Ruth responded.

But Naomi acted as if she hadn't heard Ruth. "What about Boaz?" Naomi continued. "After all, he has been kind. He would be a good husband. You know, he'll be working this evening out on the threshing floor."

"But Naomi," Ruth answered, "to be kind is one thing. To take a wife is quite another thing Are you sure this is the right way to go about getting a husband?"

Naomi explained, "In this country, when a man dies, it is the custom for his closest relative to take care of his family. Boaz is our relative. It would be natural and right for him to marry you."

Ruth finally agreed, "All right, Naomi, I'll do whatever you say."

"Listen, my daughter. Here's what you do. Take a warm bath and put on your nicest dress. Dab a little perfume behind your ears, too. Then go down to the threshing floor where Boaz is working, but don't let him see you. When he has finished his evening meal and lies down, you wait until he has fallen asleep. Then go and curl up at his feet."

That night, Boaz woke up and noticed someone lying at his feet. "Who are you?" he whispered in the darkness.

"I am Ruth, your close relative." Ruth replied. "I am here to seek your protection. I need the security of a good marriage."

"Why, Ruth! May the Lord bless you," exclaimed Boaz."Your loyalty to me is as great as your loyalty to Naomi. You are willing to marry me, instead of seeking a younger man? Everyone in Bethlehem knows you are an outstanding woman To take you as my wife would be an honor."

So Boaz and Ruth were married. And months later, a son was born to them.

Naomi was happy to become a grand-mother She exclaimed, "Ruth, you have been a greater blessing to me than seven sons. This little grandchild makes me feel young again!"

Naomi's neighbors said, "We think you should name this boy 'Obed'. Perhaps he will be famous someday" (And Obed did become the grandfather of Israel's greatest king, King David.)

Ruth had been loyal toward Naomi in spite of her own sadness and grief. She had followed Naomi to Israel and worked hard to start a new life for both of them. Then Boaz showed kindness to Ruth.

He took care of her and loved her. Ruth became a mother. She will be remembered as the great-grandmother of a good and mighty king, and as a woman who was a true friend.

You can find the story of Ruth in the Old Testament
in the book of Ruth.

HANNAH

A Woman Who Kept Her Promise to God

By Marlee Alex

Illustrated by Juan Ramón Alonso

HANNAH

A Woman Who Kept Her Promise to God

By Marlee Alex

Illustrated by Juan Ramón Alonso

"I think I need some water to make more clay bricks!" Elkanah called to his young wife. "Let's go to the river together, Hannah."

Hannah dropped the load of straw she was carrying. "You're just looking for an excuse to go swimming," she laughed.

Elkanah swept Hannah close to him with one arm. They each grabbed a pottery jug and headed off, laughing and teasing each other.

The happy couple were building their own house in the hills of Ramah They were young and full of dreams. Elkanah loved the sunshine in Hannah's smile. He was determined to build a good life for her.

Elkanah and Hannah worked hard on their new home. When it was finished, they furnished it comfortably. Year after year passed. They lived contentedly, waiting patiently for signs that the first child was on the way. In the land of Israel where they lived, children were the best thing that could happen to a couple. But no children were born to Elkanah and Hannah.

At that time there were no kings ruling Israel. Instead, God wanted His people, the Israelites, to look to Him for leadership instead of to a king. But most of the people had given up trusting in Him. Elkanah and Hannah were among the few Israelites who still loved the Lord. They had looked forward to raising a houseful of children who would learn to worship God and keep His commandments.

Elkanah often thought about his neighbors, who were living like heathen. Although they, too, were Israelites, they did not worship the one true God. Elkanah's neighbors had stopped keeping God's commandments long ago. Instead they worshipped false gods made of metal and stone. They lived farther and farther from the truth of God's Word. Many of the men had taken more than one wife. They believed the more wives and children of which a man could boast to his friends, the more important he would appear.

Elkanah began to feel restless. He was faithful to the Lord, but he missed having a son or daughter to work alongside him. He thought to himself, "There will be no one to care for Hannah and me when we are old. If children are a sign of God's blessing, then what are we doing wrong?"

Elkanah compared himself to the other men whose homes were full. The more he thought about it, the worse he felt. Finally, he convinced himself that he, too, should have another wife, one who could bear children. "Just one," he thought. "No one else will think it is wrong. And I will make it up to Hannah in other ways. Hannah will always be my first love."

So Elkanah brought a second woman into his home as his wife. Her name was Peninnah As time passed, many children were born to Peninnah and Elkanah. This was all Elkanah needed to convince him he had done the right thing. But each time Hannah heard the cries of yet one more of Peninnah's newborn babies, her heart ached until she felt it would break.

Elkanah tried to be especially good and generous to Hannah. He showered her with hugs and kisses. But his attention to Hannah made Peninnah jealous. Peninnah began to make fun of Hannah whenever Elkanah was not around. Peninnah provoked Hannah at every opportunity, chipping away at her self-confidence and her faith in God. "See this sturdy lad," she would tease, taking her youngest child on her knee, "the fruit of my loins. He is Elkanah's pride and joy. And where is your fledgling, poor barren Hannah?"

Once a year, Elkanah made it a custom to take his entire family to visit the temple of the Lord at a beautiful place called Shiloh. Elkanah told his children, "We will celebrate and have a great feast, When we worship God as a family, it will draw us closer together." Each year Elkanah hoped the trip to Shiloh would help solve the growing bitterness between his two wives.

But one year, something happened which made things even worse. After worshipping at the temple, Elkanah carved the meat for the family dinner. Peninnah was chatting with her children seated around her. Elkanah gave each of them a large helping of meat.

But when he came to Hannah, who was sitting quietly alone, he felt a wave of pity for her. "What can I do to cheer Hannah up?" Elkanah asked himself "She has no children of her own with whom to celebrate." So Elkanah gave Hannah a double portion of the delicious meat. It was the only thing he could think of which might show how much he cared about her feelings.

Peninnah noticed Elkanah heap the food onto Hannah's plate. But what bothered her most was the glow of love and tenderness in Elkanah's eyes as he had served Hannah.

Peninnah could not keep quiet. "Hannah," she whined, "your plate is full, but your nest is empty! Have you no little ones to share with? We are here to worship the Lord. But your life shows none of His blessings" Peninnah smiled scornfully, and her children giggled.

Hannah turned away from the others. She lost her composure and began to sob. Everyone else fell quiet. After what seemed an eternity, Elkanah broke the silence. "Why, Hannah, don't let Peninnah upset you She was only teasing Surely, I am better to you than ten sons."

Elkanah had wanted to make Hannah feel better, but his clumsy words only proved he did not understand her. Still, Hannah fought back her tears and calmly finished dinner. Later she slipped out of the door and headed for the temple, alone. She knew there was at least One who would listen and understand.

"Lord God," Hannah prayed, "if You will answer my prayer just once and give me a son, I will give the boy back to You. He can live here at Your temple and serve You all his life." Hannah continued to pray. But her thoughts and feelings were too deep for words. Her lips kept moving, but no sound passed between them.

Eh, the priest at Shiloh, was sitting by the temple door. He was used to the sight of women at the temple But seldom did they come to pray. More often than not, the women arrived with an open wine bottle, hoping to meet Eli's two grown sons. Eli stood up and said to Hannah, "Woman! Your eyes are red from drinking too much wine. You sit and mumble like a drunken fool."

Hannah turned to face Eli, shocked by what he had said. "Oh sir, you are wrong, I have not been drinking. I have been crying my heart out to God. My eyes are red from team, not wine. Please don't accuse me of something so terrible."

Immediately Eli realized he had made a terrible mistake. He got on his knees beside Hannah at the altar. "Lord God of heaven and earth," he prayed out loud. "Fill this woman's heart with Your peace. Answer her prayers. Yes, Lord, give her what she asks for. Amen."

Eli's simple prayer comforted Hannah and renewed her faith. "Thank you for giving me your blessing, sir," she whispered.

The rest of the week at Shiloh passed quickly for Hannah, for her heart was at peace Peninnah's rude behavior and mocking children were no longer difficult to bear. "I'm not going to let anyone take the peace of God away from me," she determined. Once she returned to Ramah, though, Hannah felt her zealous prayers at the temple were distant and dim All the same, the day came when Hannah realized her prayers had indeed been answered; she was going to have a baby.

When the child was born Hannah rejoiced, "This boy is just what I asked for. His name will be Samuel, 'Asked of God,' because he is the answer to my prayers."

Little Samuel was a healthy, lively infant. He nestled close to Hannah, drinking her sweet milk as she cradled him in her arms. Hannah sang and talked to him. As he grew, she told him stories and took him for walks, carrying him on her back. She played with him and prayed for him, until at last he was an independent toddler who no longer needed her milk.

Hannah had poured much time and energy into caring for her baby boy. Her love for Samuel was very strong. But Hannah loved God even more. And she was determined to keep the promise she had made to God at the temple.

When Samuel was about three years old, during the yearly visit to Shiloh, Hannah dressed her son in a linen tunic and took him to the temple. Eli, the priest, was sitting at the door as usual.

"Do you remember me?" Hannah asked Eli. "Seel This little boy is the answer to my prayers here at the temple years ago. Samuel is everything I ever wanted, and I have come to keep my promise and give him back to God."

Hannah put Samuel's tiny hand into the old, gnarled hand of Eli Eli took Samuel into his own home and family, promising to care for Samuel and teach him to serve the Lord in the temple.

On the journey home from Shiloh, Hannah missed that little boy who had skipped along beside her. But she sang songs of praise and thanks to God as she walked with Elkanah. Her thankfulness to God, the Giver, overflowed just as it had for the gift of the child He had given her.

"God answered my prayer and gave me what I asked for," she sang. "In fact, He gave me far beyond what I asked or even imagined. Samuel is as wonderful to me as seven sons. No longer will I have to listen to others laugh at me or suffer an aching heart. Yes, those who think they are strong are made helpless. And the helpless are given strength. God is in control. One day He will send the Anointed One, a mighty King who will be honored all over the world."

Hannah kept her promise to God, and as a result, the entire nation of Israel was wonderfully blessed. The people of Israel had fallen away from the worship of God because they had no godly leader. But Samuel grew up to become one of the greatest leaders of all time.

Samuel was a judge who made decisions about government and helped people settle quarrels. He was a prophet who taught people to understand God's laws. And he was a priest who cared for their spiritual needs. Even the enemies of Israel respected Samuel and kept peace with Israel as long as he was alive. Best of all, Israelites began to worship the one true God again.

When Hannah sang of the "Anointed One, special King," there had never been a king in Israel, nor could she have had any way of knowing that one day kings would rule Israel. For it was her son, Samuel, who later anointed the first king of Israel under God's direction. Hannah's song was God's way of giving the world a promise. God promised through Hannah a time to come when His own Son, the Prince of Peace, would reign over the entire earth, and every knee would bow before Him.

Hannah kept her promise to God, and God filled her with His Spirit. Her song includes an early prophecy about Jesus Christ, the Anointed One.

HANNAH'S PRAYER

Then Hannah prayed and said:

"My heart rejoices in the LORD;
in the LORD my horn is lifted high.
My mouth boasts over my enemies,
for I delight in your deliverance.

"There is no one holy like the LORD;
there is no one besides you;
there is no Rock like our God.

"Do not keep talking so proudly
or let your mouth speak such arrogance,
for the LORD is a God who knows,
and by him deeds are weighed.

"The bows of the warriors are broken,
but those who stumbled are armed with strength.
Those who were full hire themselves out for food,
but those who were hungry hunger no more.
She who was barren has borne seven children,
but she who has had many sons pines away.

"The LORD brings death and makes alive;
he brings down to the grave and raises up.
The LORD sends poverty and wealth;
he humbles and he exalts.
He raises the poor from the dust
and lifts the needy from the ash heap;
he seats them with princes and has them inherit a
throne of honor.

"For the foundations of the earth are the LORD's;
upon them he has set the world.
He will guard the feet of his saints,
but the wicked will be silenced in darkness.

"It is not by strength that one prevails;
those who oppose the LORD will be shattered.
He will thunder against them from heaven;
the LORD will judge the ends of the earth.

"He will give strength to his king and exalt the
horn of his anointed."

You can find the story of Hannah in the Old
Testament in the first book of Samuel,
chapters 1 and 2.

SAMUEL

Judge and Prophet

By Anne de Graaf

Illustrated by José Pérez Montero

SAMUEL

Judge and Prophet

By Anne de Graaf

Illustrated by José Pérez Montero

God thinks children are extra special. He has a special place in His heart for children, no matter where they come from. Why is this? Because of the way children laugh. Because they believe when adults sometimes doubt. Because children trust what they hear.

Samuel was a little boy who trusted what he heard. When God spoke to Samuel, he believed Samuel was extra special because even when he grew up, Samuel kept on listening to God.

The story of Samuel begins before he was born. It begins with his parents, Hannah and Elkanah They wanted to have a baby very much. As the years went by, though, no baby came. So Elkanah married a second wife. Her name was Peninnah. Peninnah could have many children.

Because of this Peninnah was very mean to Hannah. "You're a useless wife! You can't even give Elkanah one baby!"

Hannah tried not to listen She knew Elkanah loved her more than Peninnah. Elkanah's love made up for Peninnah's cruelty.

Every year Elkanah took his family to Shiloh. There they prayed to God. They thanked Him for all the good things He had given them.

During the feast in Shiloh Elkanah gave Hannah twice as much meat as Peninnah. Peninnah watched him do this. Worse than the meat, she saw the look of love on Elkanah's face. "He never looks at me that way," she thought jealously.

Peninnah waited until she was alone with Hannah. Then she flew at her in anger.

"Who do you think you are? You're not so special! Just look at you! You're getting old, Hannah!"

Hannah knew what was coming. She covered her ears, but could not keep out Peninnah's screaming.

"Look at all my children! You don't have any! What will you do when you are really old? You won't have any children to care for you! Hannah, are you listening? Ha ha!" Peninnah laughed at Hannah.

Poor Hannah. She felt as if her heart were breaking. She ran away and cried. When Elkanah found her he guessed what had happened.

"Don't listen to Peninnah," he told her. "Babies aren't so important. Look at the way I love you, Hannah. Isn't that better than ten sons?"

How could Hannah tell him what she felt? She thought, "Babies are important, My wanting a baby doesn't take away from my love for him. Even Elkanah doesn't know how I feel!"

Hannah burst into tears and turned away from Elkanah. She ran to the tent where they went to pray Inside were the stone tablets with God's Ten Commandments written on them.

An old priest named Eli was in charge of this place of prayer at Shiloh. When he saw Hannah come running inside and fall on the ground, he did not know what to think.

Eli watched Hannah closely. Her lips were moving.

"O Lord," she whispered. "You know how much I want to have a baby. Please, Lord, please help me!" Hannah's tears fell onto the ground.

"Please God, if You were to give me a son, I would give him back to You. I promise. I would bring him back to Shiloh and let this priest bring him up. The boy would be Yours, please Lord!"

Eli had seen enough. The woman's eyes were red. She was mumbling to herself. "She must be drunk," he told himself. Eli had seen too many people come to Shiloh and do nothing but eat and drink. They often stumbled into the tent where Eli kept the Ten Commandments. It was his job to ask them to leave. "Only praying people should come here, not drunks like this woman," Eli sighed.

He pointed a finger at Hannah. "You there!" he called out. "I don't want drunks in here. Get out!"

Hannah looked up in surprise. "Oh, sir, I'm not drunk. My heart is broken I'm pouring out my troubles to God."

Eli took a closer look at Hannah. He could see she was deeply upset. "Go in peace," he told her. "May the Lord bless you and give you what you have asked for."

Hannah thanked Eli for his blessing. As she walked away, she felt the weight of worry and shame lift. She did not know how, but she knew everything would be all right.

After this, whenever Peninnah teased Hannah, Hannah could ignore her. This was because Hannah knew God had heard her prayers.

It did not take long for Hannah to discover she was finally going to have a baby! Oh, that was a happy day for her and Elkanah. They prayed for their baby during the months he grew inside Hannah.

The day finally came when Hannah gave birth to a healthy little boy. 'Samuel," she told Elkanah. "I want to call this baby Samuel, because that means 'God hears.' God heard my prayers and just look how much He has blessed us!"

Samuel was a special child from the moment he was born. He was the answer to their prayers. Hannah poured all her love into Samuel. She sang to him and cuddled with him.

Sometimes Peninnah still teased her, "I have many children and you only have one!"

But Hannah would say, "My son Samuel is worth more than all your children put together." Samuel was such a good boy. He could make both his mother and father laugh and smile.

As Samuel learned how to walk and talk, Hannah taught him games. She danced with her little boy until they both fell on the ground, fizzy and laughing.

"Oh Samuel, I love you so much." Hannah told him. "But God loves you even more." Samuel hugged his mother.

Samuel's mother did not forget her promise to God. She had trusted God to hear her prayers. She had promised to give her child back to God. She would trust God to take care of her son.

Many times Samuel's mother had told him, "The most important lesson you can learn is to trust and believe in God."

When Samuel was old enough to walk and talk and feed himself, his parents brought him to Shiloh. Samuel knew this meant he was a big boy. Only the big children went to Shiloh to pray.

His mother told him about an old man who lived there. "His name is Eli. Eli is a priest He's going to take care of you. I will come and visit every year."

Samuel walked toward the tent with his mother. He tugged on her hand. "How long is a year?"

Before she could answer, though, they entered the tent. Samuel heard his mother say to an old man, "Eli, remember me? You blessed my prayers when I asked God for a baby. I promised this child to God. Now he is old enough for you to take care of him and teach him about God."

Eli bent down and held out his arms to Samuel. "Welcome, little friend," he said.

Samuel thought about how his parents had told him God would take care of him no matter where he was. Samuel let Eli hug him. When he turned around, his mother was gone. "I'm not afraid," he told himself. Samuel trusted his parents and he trusted the Lord.

Dunng the years to come, Samuel saw his mother once a year. Each time she visited, she brought Samuel a new little robe.

Meanwhile, Eli taught Samuel about God's laws for His people, the Ten Commandments. He also taught Samuel about prayer.

"Prayer is talking to God," Eli said.

"If I talk to God, will God talk back to me?" Samuel asked.

"Yes. Your heart will hear Him. But only if you're listening. A long time ago when God talked to His people they heard Him with their ears."

"Doesn't He talk like that to His people anymore?" Samuel asked.

"He probably does. They don't hear Him, though, since they're not listening." Many of God's people had turned away from God. They worshiped statues instead of the Lord God.

Samuel knew what Eli meant about God's talking to his heart. He knew that feeling of being taken care of when he fell asleep at night. "I wonder," he thought to himself "If I listen to God, would I hear Him?"

One night Samuel woke up suddenly. Someone was calling him. "Samuel."

"Here I am," Samuel said. He ran to Eli. "Yes Eli. Is there something I can get for you?"

Eli sat up in bed. He looked puzzled. "No, my son. I didn't call you. Go back to sleep ."

This happened two more times. Until finally, Eli realized Samuel must be hearing God's voice. "Samuel, I'm not calling you. The Lord is calling you! Answer Him next time by saying, `Yes Lord, I'm listening." '

Samuel did this. When God spoke again, Samuel said he was listening. Then God told Samuel what was going to happen. Samuel listened and he trusted God.

The next morning, Eli asked Samuel, "So tell me, Samuel. What did the Lord say?"

Samuel swallowed hard. He knew Eli would not like to hear what was going to happen Samuel also knew that Eli had taught him to always tell the truth. The little boy sighed.

"God told me that your sons have been doing bad things. Because you did not correct them, God will punish your family."

Eli nodded. "He is the Lord. He knows what is right."

This was the first of many times when the Lord spoke to Samuel. God spoke through Samuel. God told the boy things He wanted His people to hear "Don't worship false gods," Samuel told them. "Love the one God!"

Samuel learned to love the Lord very much. He talked to God. God talked to Samuel. Samuel listened. But often when Samuel told the people what God had said, they did not want to listen.

Before long, a terrible war broke out between the Israelites and their enemies, the Philistines. The Israelites took the box with the Ten Commandments with them into battle. But the Philistines won the battle and captured the Ten Commandments!

This was bad news for everybody, but especially for Eli. He had just heard that his two sons had died in battle. When he heard the news about the Ten Commandments, it was too much for him. He fell over backwards, hit his head on a stone and died.

Now Samuel became the holy leader, the judge, over God s people.

As the years passed Samuel continued to hear God speak. He listened to God and became wiser. Samuel judged the people fairly. Often God told Samuel about things which were going to happen. This meant Samuel could talk to the people as God's prophet, as well as their judge.

Many years went by. One day, Samuel called the people together. "If you want to follow the Lord, you must change. You must pray. Say you are sorry for the times you have not listened. Say you are sorry for worshipmg other gods. Thank God for all the good things he has given you. Talk to God and let Him talk to your hearts."

The people prayed. As they were praying, the Philistines found out the Israelites were all in one place. "Now is the time to attack!" they said to one another. "The Israelites won't be able to fight back while they're praying!"

The Philistines were very wrong. It was because of prayer that God would save the Israelites.

"Samuel! What will we do?" God's people cried out. "Pray to God for us! The Phihstines are almost here. They will kill us all!"

Samuel prayed for the people. God answered his prayers. When the Philistines attacked, God filled the sky with thunder.

The thunder boomed around the heads of the Philistines. It roared through the skies! The Philistines screamed! They ran away in fear. The Israelites chased them and won a great battle that day, thanks to God and Samuel's prayers.

Samuel had a family. He and his wife had two sons. As these sons grew older, Samuel tried to teach them about God. They did not want to listen. Still, Samuel let them help him judge the people.

When Samuel judged the people, he always asked God's help. But when his sons judged the problems of the people, they asked for money. Then they always said whatever the rich people wanted to hear.

The people were not fooled. They did not trust Samuel's sons. "How could you let those cheaters judge us?" they complained to Samuel. "When you're gone, there will be no one to lead us well."

"What do you want me to do?" Samuel asked.

The crowd moved up the stairs. "We want a king! We want you to choose a king for us!"

"Yes! A king! We want a king!"

"But God is your King," Samuel told them.

The people did not listen. "All the other countries around us have kings. If we can't trust your sons to judge us fairly, then we want a king!"

Samuel sighed. "I will talk to God about this. Will you listen to what He says?" he asked.

"As long as God says we can have a king!" The people were very stubborn.

Samuel asked God, "What do You want, Lord?"

God said, "You were right to tell the people I should be their King. But since they think they can only follow My laws if they have a king, give them their king. Let them know, though, what it will cost them."

Samuel told the people what God had said. "Are you really sure you want a king? Your children will become his servants. Your sons will have to fight in his army. You will have to give him a share of your crops. God won't help you when you complain about your king!"

The people did not listen. "We want a king' We want a king!"

So Samuel sent them home. And he started waiting for God to show him who should be the first king of Israel.

Before long, God told Samuel, "Tomorrow a stranger will ask you about some lost donkeys. He is the one who will become king. Pour oil on him and bless him."

Samuel waited all day In the evening he saw a tall, handsome man walking toward the city gates. The man's name was Saul. Saul asked, "Do you know where the holy man Samuel is? I am trying to find my father's lost donkeys. I was hoping he could help me."

Samuel smiled. "I am Samuel. Your donkeys have already been found. I'm on my way to a feast on top of this hill. The people there are worshiping Got" Samuel pointed up the hill. "Come join me and you can sit at the head of the table." Saul did not know why Samuel should pay him such an honor. But he said yes and followed Samuel up the hill.

When Saul left the next day, Samuel walked with him to the edge of the city. Then he stopped the big man. "God has a message for you, Saul." Saul's eyes grew big.

Samuel said, "The Lord has chosen you to become the fast king of Israel."

Saul gasped. "Me? But I come from the smallest family in the smallest tribe. I'm no one important!"

"You are now," Samuel told him. "Now bow your head and I will bless you in God's name."

Saul bowed his head. Samuel poured oil on Saul This was a sign that God had chosen Saul and would help him to be a good king.

"Go back to your father so he doesn't worry."Samuel said. He told Saul where he could find his father's donkeys. He told him to wait until he was called to become king.

Saul heard Samuel, but did not really understand.

A short time later Samuel called the people together. "God will show you who your king is," he said. Then, out of all the tribes, God chose Saul's tribe. Out of all the families, God chose Saul's family. Out of all the men, God chose Saul.

"Saul? Who is Saul?" the people cried. "Where's this Saul?"

Samuel asked God. The Lord told him that Saul was hiding between all the baskets.

The people ran and found Saul They brought him to Samuel. "There is your king!" Samuel pointed.

"Oh, he's so tall and handsome. Yes, he will make a good king! Long live Saul) Long live Saul!"

At first Saul was a good king. He listened when Samuel told him what God said. But then, slowly but surely, Saul started doing what he wanted, instead of what God wanted.

He grew proud. "I'm a great king," he often thought. "Tell me I'm a great king," he ordered his servants.

"You are a great king," they told him But Samuel warned Saul to be careful. "You should not be so proud of yourself." Saul ignored Samuel's advice.

All this time the Israelites were still fighting wars against their enemies. During one of these battles, Saul did something very bad. He tried to be king without God. He did just what he wanted to Stead of what God had told him to do.

Samuel had told Saul, "God wants you to kill every one of these enemies Destroy all

their animals and treasures." Saul had his orders from God But did he listen? No. Instead, when Saul saw how rich this enemy tribe was, he stole their animals and treasures for his army. And he chose not to kill their king.

God was sad that Saul had not listened again. So God was sorry He had made Saul king. He sent Samuel to warn Saul that he had done something very wrong by not doing what God had ordered.

Even then Saul would not listen. Instead, he made excuses. "We thought we could use the animals as sacrifices to God But it's not really my fault. My army did it. I didn't do it."

Samuel knew Saul was lying. "The Lord says He would rather you had listened to Him than offer animals for sacrifices. Because you've become so proud, He doesn't want you to be the king anymore." Saul knew he had made a terrible mistake.

God sent Samuel to find the man who would become king after Saul. Samuel traveled to Bethlehem. There he visited a man named Jesse When Samuel met Jesse's sons, he asked God which one would become the new king. "The eldest is very handsome, Lord," Samuel said.

"I don't look at a person's outside beauty," God said. "I look at the heart."

Samuel asked if there were no other sons. Jesse sent for his youngest boy. He was taking care of the sheep. "This is David," Jesse said.

God told Samuel, "This is the one." Samuel poured oil over David's head. This was a sign that God was blessing him in a very special way and that someday he would become king.

At that time, David was just a boy who loved God in his heart very much. In many ways he was just like Samuel had been when he was a boy They both knew how to pray to God and listen for answers in their hearts.

In the years to come, Samuel learned how wise a choice God had made. David proved how much he trusted God by fighting the giant Goliath. David was so brave, Saul made him the captain of his army.

One time when Saul and David were riding back from a battle side by side. Women danced around them and sang, "Saul has killed thousands, but David has killed his tens of thousands!"

This made Saul very angry He was still king, but ever since Samuel had told him God would choose another king, Saul had felt jealous and troubled Samuel had warned Saul, but he had not listened. Now it was too late.

Saul's anger turned him into a mean man. As time went by, he could not stop thinking of how jealous he was of David. Nothing Samuel said could change Saul's mind.

Finally, even though David was his best fighter, Saul tried to kill him. So David ran away to Samuel.

"The king thinks I want to take his place. He's wrong," David told Samuel. "I will listen to Saul as long as God wants me to. I was in the throne room when he suddenly picked up his spear and threw it at me! Why Samuel? Why does the king hate me so much?"

Samuel was a very, very old man by this time. He sighed. "You listen to the Lord in your heart, David. This is why God chose you. Someday He will make you king. Saul knows you are special and wants that for himself."

Samuel took David's young hands in his old hands. "You must run away from Saul and keep yourself safe, David. Never forget, though, to ask God what you should do Listen to His answers and you will stay as special to Him as you were when you were a boy."

David hid from Saul for many years. During this time, Samuel grew so old that he finally died. When Samuel died, he went to heaven.

Samuel was the last judge of Israel. And he was the first prophet for Israel. All his life he had prayed for God's people. While Saul chased David, Samuel prayed for David God heard Samuel's prayers After Samuel's death, Saul was killed in battle and David became the greatest king Israel ever had.

All that Samuel had said would happen, did happen. . . because he trusted what he heard God say.

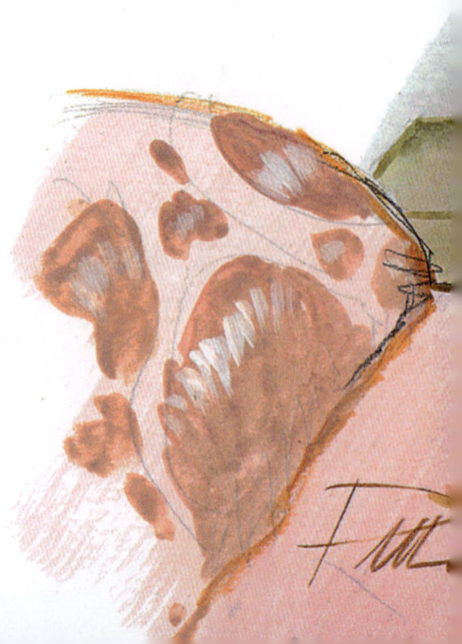

You can find the story of Samuel in the Old Testament
in the book of First Samuel, chapters 1–25.

DAVID

The Brave Shepherd Boy Who Became a Great King

By Ben Alex

Illustrated by François Davot

F.D.

DAVID

The Brave Shepherd Boy Who Became a Great King

By Ben Alex

Illustrated by François Davot

It was lovely in the green hills outside Bethlehem.

From the top of the hill where the shepherd boy sat, he could see many miles away. Below, the lush fields lay like a great carpet over the valley. Off to the right, the houses of Bethlehem were clustered around the marketplace. They looked like a heap of square rocks in the sunshine. To the left the sheep spread out, grazing on the slope below.

Suddenly a shout broke the silence of the hills and echoed throughout the valley,

"David! David!"

The shepherd boy spun around. He had a tanned face, sparkling dark eyes, black curly hair, and strong limbs. His brother Eliab came running up the hill.

"David! Hurry back home!"

"Why? Is anything wrong?" asked David, waiting for his brother to catch his breath.

"You'll...have to...come..right away!" Eliab panted. "Samuel, the prophet, has come to visit."

"What? Why would Samuel come to Bethlehem? Who's in trouble?"

"It could be your answered Eliab. "Samuel wants to see you!" Whenever Samuel wanted to see people it usually meant they had sinned and were in trouble.

David's eyes bulged in surprise. "Why me?" Eliab explained, "I don't know. The prophet just looked at each one of us Then he shook his head and asked Jesse, our father, Don't you have any more sons?" So Father sent me to fetch you!"

Eliab turned and galloped off down the hill. David followed close at his heels.

David's seven brothers stood lined up in the farmyard In front of them, the famous prophet Samuel was leaning on his staff. Nobody said a word. They all were waiting for David.

"Here he comes!" exclaimed Jesse.

David slipped into the end of the line. Being the youngest, he was used to being

last and being teased and talked down to. "You're only a child!" his brothers often taunted. Then they would tickle him or laugh behind his back. Sometimes they called him nasty names then knocked him on the back of the head. How David hated it! He longed to grow up and become big like his brothers. But today they did not tease him. They just wondered what terrible things he had done to deserve a visit from Samuel.

David wondered the same. Why did Samuel the prophet want to see him?

Samuel's piercing eyes fell upon David. He squinted, then a trace of a smile brightened his eyes.

"He's the one!" Samuel's hoarse voice announced.

David began to tremble. "Which one?" he mumbled. Then he saw Samuel pull out a bull horn and fill it with oil The prophet was going to anomt somebody! In Israel a man was anointed with oil when he was to be used by God in a special way. The last person Samuel had anointed was King Saul.

Surprise filled the eyes of David's older brothers. Did it mean one of them was to become a disciple of Samuel or some other kind of important leader?

Samuel poured the holy oil over David's head. Everybody held their breath. David was thinking, "Why me? I'm only a shepherd boy." David's brothers were thinking the same thing.

The oldest brother, Eliab, thought, "I'm older and stronger than David."

The next brother, Abinadab, thought, "I'm smarter than David."

The next brother, Shammah, thought, "I'm better looking." Each of Jesse's sons had a good reason for thinking he should be the one to be anointed instead of David.

But Samuel did not even give them a second glance. He just nodded goodbye to Jesse and said, "The Lord doesn't look at the outside of someone. He looks at the heart." Then he turned on his heel and left as suddenly as he had come.

As David went back to his flock of sheep, his brothers stared after him. Their youngest brother had been anointed by the prophet, chosen by God to become His special servant! How could this be?

F.DAVOT

At that time there were rumors of war in the land of Israel. Some people said the Philistines were gathering an army to fight against Israel. Israel had known many enemies, but the Philistines were the worst.

David's three oldest brothers, Eliab, Abinadab, and Shammah, were soldiers in the army of Israel. Sometimes they came home on leave and talked about how proud they were to be soldiers.

"Now tell me," said Jesse during one of their visits, "is it true what they say about the king? I've heard he has become grumpy and moody. They say his own family is afraid of him. Some even say he has gone crazy."

"There's something to it, Father," Eliab said sadly. "King Saul is suspicious and jealous of everyone. Nobody is safe around him anymore."

"Yes," continued Abinadab. "He sits for days and stares into space. The morale of the soldiers is getting worse and worse."

Jesse sighed. "I wonder what's going to become of Israel? Things are not what they used to be."

"Just leave it to us, Father," said Shammah. "We are soldiers now. We'll crush the Philistines."

"I want to become a soldier, too," beamed David. He loved to listen to his brothers' reports from the battlefield. However, he had to stay home and take care of his father's sheep.

"Sure," laughed the brothers, "you're still just a baby."

"Hey dreamer," they added. "Made up any new sheep songs lately?"

That same morning, as David was playing his lyre in the hayloft, there was a pounding on the gate. It was a messenger from King Saul himself with a request for Jesse. Jesse could hardly believe his own ears.

"The king requests your youngest son, David to come right away to the palace and make music for the king."

David was scared and excited at the same time. As he left, his seven brothers stood at the gate, scratching their heads. David, their youngest brother, requested by the king? Now they were not laughing.

"Bye," smiled David. Then he rode off with the king's messenger.

King Saul sat on his throne and waited for the new musician. His General Abner had advised Saul to listen to good music. "It would make you feel better," Abner assured him.

Saul did not even notice when David entered the room He just sat there and stared into space. His eyes were lifeless. He looked tired and worried. His face was pale like that of a dead man. David cleared his throat and began to sing.

The music filled the rooms of the royal palace as it had the hills of Bethlehem. It spoke of the quietness of the fields, the simple life of the shepherd, the happiness of those who put their trust in God.

David trusted God. Even though he had often wondered what it was that God had chosen him for, he was patiently waiting for God to lead him.

Slowly Saul's eyes began to brighten. Color and expression returned to his pale face. He turned toward the new musician and whispered hoarsely, "Go on! I like that!"

David continued, "The Lord is my Shepherd, I shall not want.. ." The music was like weightless butterflies fluttering in the king's room.

From then on, Saul often asked David to play the lyre and sing for him. He started to look much better. He even began to smile. He had guests come eat around his table. Then, suddenly, the happy days came to an end.

Runners arrived from the valley of Elah.

"The Philistine army has marched into the other side of the valley," they reported. "They could attack any time. Saul, you are needed to lead your men."

So, Saul hurried off to his army at Elah.

And David returned to his home in Bethlehem.

David liked being back home. He had missed his sheep and the hills where he made his songs and talked to God But he often thought back to the time when he had played for King Saul. He dreamed the king would someday send for him again. He still did not realize that God was preparing him for something more.

Each evening at sunset, when David brought his flock of sheep back to the sheepfold, the sheep would crowd through the narrow opening in the stone wall. David called each one by name. Then, when all were safe inside, he would spread his skin mattress in front of the doorway and lay watching the stars before he fell asleep. He became the door to the sheepfold. No one could come in and harm his lambs Until one night ...

"Grrraaaaugh!" It was a frightening roar! David shot three feet into the air and landed on his feet. For a moment he stood paralyzed. Only his eyes moved. S-l-o-w-l-y he turned his head and looked right into the eyes of a...lion!

The animal stood on top of the stone wall. Its huge body was bathed in the moonlight. David had goose bumps all over, even in his hair. In a minute the lion would jump down and devour either him or one of his lambs. Without a sound David reached down and searched with his hand for his rod. He did not take his eyes off the lion for even a second. And then.. .

David shot into the air like a cat going for its prey. He landed on the back of the lion and forced the rod towards the soft point under the lion's throat, pulling with all his might. The lion stiffened for a second He growled once, then collapsed, limp as a rag. He slid down the wall and rolled over on its side.

It was dead! David had broken the lion's neck!

That night it took a long time for David to fall asleep "Thank You, God," he whispered. "I know I couldn't have done this by myself Thank You for giving me strength to kill the lion!"

F. DAVOT

At breakfast the next morning David told his family what had happened. His brothers shook their heads doubtfully, "Killed a lion? David? How would he do something like that?" They chuckled under their breath. They had sometimes believed his stories about killing bears. But he had killed them from a distance with his slingshot After all, David was good with a sling. They could admit that. But breaking the neck of a lion? That was beyond belief.

"It wasn't really me," said David. "God did it."

"God?" laughed his brothers. But when they went outside to examine the dead lion on the ground, they stopped laughing.

Without saying another word, they went off to work.

Jesse was proud of his youngest son. "Well done, David!" he exclaimed. "You deserve a day off. I want you to go to where your other brothers are stationed at Elah. They'll be needing some more food. Look for them in the front line of King Saul's army."

"Oh, I was hoping you'd say that, Father!" shouted David as he lifted his father up in the air. He could hardly wait to see the king's army for himself.

King Saul's army was lined up on the eastern slope of the valley of Elah. The Philistine army was posted on the western slope. But what a difference! The Israelites looked more like farmers out on a hunt than soldiers at war Only a few of them had any real armor or weapons. Most Israelites carried rods and homemade stone weapons. But the Philistine army carried iron weapons and shields. They wore bronze helmets.

David elbowed his way through the rods and spears and legs of his countrymen. He wanted to see his three brothers on the front line. Suddenly someone hit him on the back of his head. He swayed and spun around.

"David, What are you doing here? This is the king's army! Aren't you supposed to be tending sheep?" Eliab looked angry.

"Father sent me.. ."

"Don't make things up," interrupted

Abinadab. "You came to watch the battle, didn't you?" Then he grabbed David by the shoulder and pushed him. David staggered three steps backwards and landed flat on his back.

"Can't I even explain?" he yelled. "I'm your brother. I've come with supplies for you, and you treat me like dirt!" Then he stood up and walked off.

Just at that moment something happened which made the entire army of Israel tremble in their sandals. David stopped and stared.

A soldier emerged from the ranks of the Philistine army. He was huge! Absolutely gigantic! David stopped breathing as he watched him. The giant walked out into the middle of the valley and stopped. He looked like an enormous bronze statue with helmet and full-scale coat of armor. A bronze javelin was slung across his back. In his hand he held a spear the size of a boat mast. His shield bearer standing at his side looked like a dwarf in comparison.

"All that must weigh at least two hundred pounds!" gasped David. He turned to the nearest Israelite. "Who is this man? Has he come out to fight all by himself?"

"He's Goliath from Gath," stammered the Israelite soldier. "The Philistines think we should settle this war with a contest between the giant and an Israelite. For the last forty days he has come out to challenge us. But nobody dares fight against him."

"I don't blame them," mumbled David.

David kept his eye on the giant. The man looked like a monster, not a human being, he was so tall! Then the giant lifted his arm. The Israelites shivered as he bellowed, "Listen, you slaves of Israel! Where is the man who wants to fight me? If he can kill me, we'll all surrender to you. But if I kill him, you must surrender to us." Then Goliath thumbed his nose at the Israelites and yelled, "Today I defy the ranks of Israel!"

David was shocked! His chin dropped. His knuckles went white, he clenched his shepherd's rod so tightly. He could not believe anyone would dare defy the people of God. David's eyes riveted onto the giant as he said slowly but firmly, "Will somebody bring me before the king? I'll fight the giant!"

King Saul looked at David He did not recognize his former musician Then he looked at the giant. A wry smile crept over his face. "You can't fight the giant," the king said. You don't even know what you're doing."

David tried to ignore Saul's words. "I'm not afraid of that ungodly Philistine!" he answered.

"How old are you?" the king asked.

"I'm sixteen. Sixteen-and-a-half."
"And you want me to believe you can fight giants?"

"I've killed bears and lions before!"

King Saul thought for a minute. Then he said, "All right, go ahead. You may fight the Philistine since nobody else will."

F. DAVOT

Saul insisted David put on his own royal armor. He loaded his weapons into David's hands. David looked like a little boy playing soldier. The king's helmet kept falling down over his eyes.

"This won't work," David finally said. "I'll fight the giant my way!" He took off the royal armor. Then he went to meet Goliath from Gath.

But his brothers were angry. They stared after him as if to say, "That's it! See now, what this crazy little brother of ours has got us into!"

But David kneeled down and picked up five smooth stones. Then he pulled out the sling from his belt. In the other hand he held his rod and walked down into the valley.

Now it was the giant's turn to be shocked. "What do you think I am?" he shouted at David. "A dog? I asked for a proper soldier, and out steps a shepherd lad armed with a rod! I'll turn you into vulture food!"

Goliath took three giant steps forward.

"That's what you think!" David yelled back. "You come against me with all your fancy armor. But I come against you in the name of the Lord! He is the God of the army of Israel whom you've defied. Today the Lord will give you into my hands,"

David was only fifty feet away from the giant. He reached into his bag, took out a stone, and placed it in the sling. Taking aim at the giant's forehead, right between the eyes, he pictured the stone smashing through Goliath's skull.

"God," he whispered, "help me aim steady and make my stone fly straight." Then he whirled the sling over his head and sent the stone whining through the air.

"Smack!" The stone hurled through the air and was right on target. For a minute Goliath tottered cross-eyed. Then he gave a yelp, stumbled forward and thudded onto the ground like som giant tree trunk.

"Whommm !"

David could feel the ground shake beneath his feet.

There was total silence The soldiers on both sides tiptoed forward to find out what had happened. David ran straight up to Goliath and pulled out the giant's sword. He raised it high over his head.

"Zaapppp!" The giant's head went rolling David grasped it by the hair and held it up in the air. Suddenly the eastern side of the valley turned into a tumultuous wave of people, all roaring. The Israelites poured into the valley and up the other side, running after the terrified Philistines.

They chased them all the way back to Gath and Ekron. What a battle! What a day! The army of Israel blotted out the ungodly Philistines. It was all thanks to a shepherd boy who dared to answer the challenge of a giant defying Israel and their God.

That evening, before David left the valley of Elah, he kneeled down at the very spot where he had killed the giant. He prayed, "Thank You God, for giving victory to Your people!"

David had become a national hero. Rumors about the young giant-killer spread like wildfire throughout the land of Israel. "We want David as our king!" cheered the people as the army triumphantly returned home. This made King Saul even more jealous and angry. He was afraid David would take his kingdom away from him.

But David did not want to fight or hurt Saul. David respected him as the true leader and king of Israel. "Lord God," David prayed, "I pray for peace in our land, and that Saul and I might live in peace."

But this was not possible since there was a war raging inside Saul's own heart. He envied David. He felt threatened by him, and felt he had no choice but to kill his young soldier. He hunted David mercilessly.

F. DAVOT

David was forced to run away from Saul. Six hundred brave soldiers followed him. "We will help you defeat Saul," they offered. But David was firm "If God wants to take away the kingdom from Saul," he answered, "He doesn't need our help. We'll wait and see."

David and his six hundred men hid in the wilderness, in caves, and in the small forests of Israel. Once they were forced to hide in a neighboring enemy country. Saul chased them from one end of the land to the other.

One day some terrible news arrived at David's hideout. It hit David like a stunning blow. King Saul was dead!

He had been killed in another great battle against the Philistine army. Many of his sons were dead too. David wept over Saul and his sons. The country was torn apart. Some people remained loyal to Saul's only surviving son. But half the country claimed David as their new king.

Seven years had passed since David killed Goliath. Another seven years would go by before David became king of a united Israel. What a glorious day that was!

It was not until this day that David realized the importance of what the old prophet Samuel had done so many years ago, when he had anointed him at home in Bethlehem. The anointing had been God's promise that someday He would make David king of Israel.

"Hail the king! Hail King David!" the crowds cheered.

David set up his kingdom in the great city of Jerusalem He built a magnificent castle right in the center He conquered the enemies around Israel, and brought the lost Ark of the Covenant back from the land of the Philistines who had captured it long before. David wanted Israel to only worship the one, true God.

David ruled for many years. God made David another promise, "Your kingdom will last forever!"

"How can this be?" wondered David. One thousand years after David's death, Jesus, the Savior of the world, was born in Bethlehem, the town of David. He was a direct descendant of King David.

Jesus came to establish a kingdom of peace which would have no end. This kingdom lives on even today, within the hearts of those who believe in Him.

F. DAVOT

You can find the story of David in the Old Testament
from the book of First Samuel, chapter 16 to the book of First Kings, chapter 2.

ELIJAH

Prophet of Fire

By Anne de Graaf

Illustrated by José Pérez Montero

ELIJAH

Prophet of Fire

By Anne de Graaf

Illustrated by José Pérez Montero

A very long time ago there lived a wicked queen. Her name was Jezebel. She was married to the Israelite king Ahab. Jezebel was very evil and very powerful. There was only one man who dared to fight Jezebel. This brave man was called Elijah.

Elijah had been chosen by God to speak His words to His people, the Israelites This meant Elijah was a prophet for God.

Jezebel did not even believe in God. She came from a people who worshiped statues of false gods. The Lord God had ordered His people to pray to no one but Him. When King Ahab married Jezebel, he started worshiping her false gods instead. This was very, very wrong. It broke God's fiist Commandment to His people, that they should only worship the one true God.

Evil Queen Jezebel even tried to kill the Lord's prophets. Then she told Ahab to make his people stop praying to God. "Tell them I have killed all their prophets! Tell them they must worship my gods!"

Ahab did whatever his wife wanted. He built places to worship Jezebel's false gods. He made the people pray and burn sacrifices there. And the people did what their king wanted.

Because of this terrible thing, Jezebel and Ahab became known as the most evil king and queen God's people ever had.

Everyone was very afraid of Jezebel, everyone except Elijah. Jezebel always tried to kill her enemies. When she tried to kill the prophets of the Lord, though, at least one man escaped That one man was Elijah.

Elijah knew Jezebel would be hunting him. Yet he felt God pushing him to speak with Ahab. Elijah was God's prophet. It was his job to tell people what God wanted them to hear.

Elijah went to the royal palace. There he warned Ahab, "You must stop worshiping these false gods. You've made the people stop praying to God. He will punish you for this!"

Ahab swallowed. "I was just doing what my wife told me. There's nothing wrong with the people praying to statues. Who could it harm? God won't notice."

But God had noticed. Elijah told him, "The Lord God is going to make your land dry up like a desert, He will not let the rain fall again until I ask Him to!" Then Elijah left the palace.

God told Elijah to hide in the hills. Elijah was alone, but God took care of him. Elijah drank water from a nearby stream. When he was hungry, big black birds called ravens brought him food. Every day the ravens brought Elijah meat and bread.

While the rest of the country was going hungry and thirsty, Elijah had plenty to eat and drink. This lasted a long time, until one day, the stream finally dried up.

When there was no more water in the stream, Elijah asked God what he should do. The Lord told him, “Go to a village near the place where Jezebel comes from. You will find a woman whose husband is dead. She will give you food.”

Elijah did as God told him. He looked very strange as he entered the village. Many people stared at Elijah. He had been living for months in the desert and looked like a wild man! His hair was long and he wore animal skins as his clothes.

When he spoke to the widow, though, she did not run away. “Would you please give me a little water and some bread?” he asked her.

The woman shook her head sadly. “I have nothing.” She looked down at the fire-wood in her arms “I was gomg to use this wood to make a fire for my last meal. My son and I have nothing left but a little flour and oil. I was going to make a little bread from that.

That will be our last meal, and then we will starve to death." The woman did not look up.

Elijah asked God what he could do. God told him. Elijah said softly, "Don't be afraid. Make the bread. Then give some to me. The Lord God will make sure your flour and oil do not run out until He sends rain to this place again."

It had been a very long time since there was any rain. Even King Ahab and Queen Jezebel did not have enough to drink But they still refused to believe God could help them.

When this woman heard Elijah's promise, she could hardly believe her ears. "How is it possible?" she asked herself. Unlike Ahab and Jezebel, though, she chose to believe God could help her "Yes," she nodded to Elijah. "Yes, come home with me and I will feed you."

She did not know how it had happened, but the widow believed the promise this strange man of God had made to her.

That evening, when the flour and oil were almost all gone, her son shouted, "Mother! Mother! Look, the jar is full of oil again! And the bowl of flour is full, too! Didn't you say it was all gone?"

The woman smiled. "This is a miracle. That man of God said it would happen like this."

Elijah came down the stairs and heard her. "Listen to your mother," he said to the boy. "It is a miracle, God's way of taking care of people when they listen and believe."

From that day on, there was always oil in the jar and flour in the bowl Day after day the woman had enough food for her son and for Elijah. The prophet came to live with the widow and she fed him and gave him a place to sleep.

Elijah had no family of his own. As he stayed with the widow and her son, he grew fond of the boy. He prayed for him and taught him about the Lord.

Then one day, the widow's son became very sick. He had been starving to death before Elijah came to live with him and his mother. So he was already very weak when he became ill.

Now the boy grew weaker and weaker. Finally he died in his mother's arms. The woman had already lost her husband. Now her son was dead.

She cried out to Elijah, "Why? Why me? You said your God would take care of us. Why am I being punished? Look at my son! He's dead!"

"Here, give him to me," Elijah said. He gently took the boy into his own arms. Elijah carved the boy upstairs to his room, while the mother stayed downstairs, sobbing.

Elijah laid the boy on his own bed. Then he leaned over him and prayed. "Dear God, have You brought so much sadness into this home, where I am staying?"

Elijah did a very strange thing. He stretched himself out on the boy three times. He prayed, "My Lord God, let this boy's life come back to him!" Three times Elijah begged God to make the boy live agam. He asked God with all his heart.

And then, suddenly, Elijah felt the boy's body growing warmer under him. He gasped and looked at the child's face. His eyes fluttered open. The boy looked at Elijah. Then he smiled!

"You're alive," Elijah whispered to his little friend. He held him close and said a prayer of thanks to God. The Lord had heard Elijah's cries The boy was alive!

Elijah picked up the boy again and brought him to his mother. "Look, your son Is alive"

The mother wiped the tears from her eyes. She shivered. "No, but," she started to say. Then she saw her son smiling at her.

Again she started crying. This time these were happy tears. As she put her arms around Elijah and her boy, the woman said, "Now I know you are a man of God. The messages you speak from God are the truth. Just look, my son is alive!"

Elijah stayed with the widow and her son for three years All that time the rest of the country grew drier and drier. It had been a very long time since any rain had fallen. The land became a desert. Many people had no food. No one had any water. All the rivers and streams and lakes had dried up. The only water was in the sea, and they could not drink that.

As the years without rain dragged on, Jezebel grew more and more furious. "This is all your fault!" the evil queen yelled at her husband.

Ahab sent soldiers to comb the country for Elijah. Meanwhile Queen Jezebel had again ordered her soldiers to kill all the Lord's prophets "That will teach their God to dry up our land!" Only a hundred managed to escape.

When Elijah was finally found, Ahab went to see him. He said, "You troublemaker, Elijah! Thanks to you, there's been no rain for three years!"

"I am not the troublemaker," Elijah said. "You are. You chose to worship Jezebel's gods. The Lord sent no rain so you would learn He is the one and only God. Now I will show you how worthless your false gods are! Bring eight hundred of Jezebel's priests to the top of Mount Carmel. There we will have a contest!"

A few days later Ahab and Jezebel's priests arrived for the contest. A huge crowd of Israelites were watching. Elijah told them, "Now you will have to choose between the Lord God and Baal, Watch and see if Baal can set on fire the wood and bull you have offered in front of his statue. Just see if he listens!"

The priests of Baal danced and prayed and sang and yelled and even cut themselves. But no fire fell from heaven.

Elijah laughed at Baal's priests, "Maybe you should shout louder' This god of yours might be thinking, or busy or traveling or sleeping! Ha, ha!"

Still nothing happened. Then it was Elijah's turn. Elijah turned to the people. "Do you know why nothing happened? Because Baal is a nothing god! God wants to prove to you that He alone is God, there is no one else!"

Elijah set up his own offering to the Lord. He repaired the Lord's altar which Jezebel's priests had destroyed. He dug a hole around the altar and laid stones around the trench. He placed the wood and dead bull on top of the altar.

Then Elijah poured four jars of water onto the altar! He did this three times. The people gasped, "How can it possibly catch fire now that it is wet?"

Elijah heard them. "Now you will know God is the only God No one but the Lord could light this with fire now that I have soaked it in water."

Elijah started praying. "Lord God, show these people that You are the true God of Israel. Send fire from heaven, I pray!"

Then, with a mighty "swoosh!" fire rained down from the sky! The water-soaked wood and meat were burned in a mighty fire The crowd shouted, "The Lord is God! The Lord is God!" Elijah cried out,

"Now do you believe that only the Lord is the true God?"

The people had fallen to their knees. "Yes, yes, we believe!" Elijah told the people to capture Jezebel's priests so he could kill them all.

Once he had done that, Elijah prayed for rain. Again he wanted to show the Israelites how powerful God was. Again, God answered Elijah's prayers. Soon rain fell on the thirsty land.

The people raised their hands and cheered. At last, once they believed in God, He had sent them rain!

Elijah hoped with all his heart that the people would remember what they had seen that day.

Later, wicked Jezebel heard what had happened on Mount Carmel. "He did what?" she screamed at Ahab. "He killed my priests? Well, you tell Elijah that now I'm going to kill him!"

When Elijah heard about Jezebel's threat, he ran for his life. Before he left the city, though, he saw a group of women worshiping one of Jezebel's false gods. "Oh Lord, they've forgotten You already!" Elijah cried.

He hid in the desert and felt very tired and upset. An angel of the Lord came to give him food and water. “Rest, and you will feel better,” the angel said.

Then Elijah traveled deeper into the desert until he reached a cave. There he fell to the ground, very afraid and very sad.

Elijah fell asleep inside the cave. He felt lost and alone. Suddenly, he heard the Voice of God say, "Elijah, why are you here?"

Elijah woke up with a start. "Oh Lord, I knew You would hear my prayers I've tried my hardest to show Your people they should only pray to You. But no matter how many miracles happen, they still won't listen. Jezebel has killed Your prophets I'm all alone. And now she wants to kill me, tool" Elijah had lost all hope.

The Lord said, "I want you to wait for Me. I will pass by you and make you feel stronger." This was an amazing thing! The Lord Himself was going to appear to Elijah!

So Elijah waited. First came a mighty wind. It blasted through the mountains and split the rocks apart. But the Lord was not in the wind. Then came a frightening earthquake. But the Lord was not in the earthquake.

Then came a fire which burnt everything for miles around. But the Lord was not in the fire.

And then, as soft as a breeze, there came the sound of a gentle whisper. Elijah looked up. He covered his face with his cloak and walked out to the entrance of the cave.

Elijah complained again to the Lord. "The people won't listen! I'm all alone! And now Jezebel wants to kill me, tool" He thought his life was almost over.

The Lord had plans for Elijah, though. "No, Elijah, your life is not almost over. Rest for a while in the desert. Then go to Damascus.

There I will show you your helper, a young man named Elisha. Then you won't be so alone."

This made Elijah feel much better. He smiled. The Lord had known just what Elijah most needed, a helper.

So Elijah stayed in the desert for a while. Then he traveled to Damascus and did as God had told him. He went looking for Elisha.

Even though the two men had names which sounded alike, they were different. Elijah was much older than Elisha. Elijah was a wild-looking prophet who wandered the land telling people about God.

Elisha was a farmer. When Elijah found Elisha, he was plowing a field with a pair of oxen. Elijah called to him. He put his cloak around Elisha's shoulders. It was a way of showing Elisha he had been chosen to follow and learn from Elijah.

Elisha knew what it meant. "Please, may I say good-bye to my parents? Then I will follow you." Elijah agreed as Elisha told his friends and family about the exciting thing which had happened to him.

In the years to come Elisha was a great help to Elijah He took care of Elijah. And he watched and learned from him, so that someday, Elisha would be able to become a prophet for the Lord, just like Elijah.

All this time the wicked queen Jezebel was still causing trouble. She continued to make her husband Ahab force the Israelites to worship her false gods. And Jezebel swore that if she ever did find Elijah, she would kill him!

Elijah knew this, but he was not afraid. Now he had young Elisha at his side. The Lord had made Elijah stronger. Together, the two men wandered the country telling people not to listen to Jezebel.

"Her gods are nothing. Pray to the Lord God instead. He loves you and wants to help you, but you must believe in Him and not these statues!" Some people listened, but very few believed.

By now, Ahab was a very selfish king. Whenever he saw something he wanted, he took it. This happened once when King Ahab saw a vineyard he wanted. It was right next to the palace. He called the owner, a man named Naboth.

"Sell me your vineyard I want it!"

"I cannot sell you that land. It belonged to my father and my grandfather and before that, to his father," Naboth said.

But Ahab would not listen. He went home and complained to the queen She laughed at him and told him, "Don't worry! I'll make sure you get your vineyard."

Ahab's evil wife did just that. She paid two men to tell lies about Naboth She had him arrested. These two men made up horrible stories about Naboth. Finally the men of the city dragged Naboth out to the city walls and stoned him to death.

Once poor Naboth was dead, Jezebel sent for Ahab. “I’ve had that man killed, the one who would not sell you his land. Now you can have his vineyard.” Jezebel laughed.

Thanks to Jezebel’s lies, Ahab had what he wanted. But God had seen how a good man had been killed. He sent Elijah to talk to the king.

“The Lord has seen how Jezebel murdered a man so you could steal his land,” Elijah told Ahab. Ahab turned pale “The Lord says that when you and your family die, the dogs will lick up your blood.”

Ahab knew he had done something very evil. But Elijah was not finished He knew that if Jezebel found him near the palace she would surely have him killed. But he was not afraid. The Lord had given Elijah a message for Ahab. Elijah had spent his whole life speaking God’s words to people. He wasn’t about to stop now.

“And when Jezebel dies, she will be eaten by dogs, here right near her own palace. That is the Lord’s punishment for you and your wife.” Ahab realized what a terrible thing he had done and felt very sorry, but it was too late.

Much later, while Ahab was fighting in a battle, he was hit by an arrow. He died while riding m his chariot. After Ahab was buried, a soldier was cleaning the king’s chariot when he noticed some dogs licking up Ahab’s blood Everything Elijah had said would happen, came true.

During this time Israel was fighting many battles against many tribes. King Ahab died during a battle against Aram. But Israel was also fighting against another country where God's own people were living, called Judah. This was tragic. Two of the twelve tribes of God's people who should have been worshiping the same God were killing each other.

Again, though, it was because Jezebel and Ahab were such wicked leaders. Over and over again they had made the Israelites fight battles against other tribes, including their own people! Most of the time it was because they wanted more treasure or land, because they were so selfish.

When Ahab died in battle, his son Ahaziah became king. Ahaziah was even more evil than his father. He did everything his wicked mother told him to. And Ahaziah was never sorry.

But the worst thing about Ahaziah was that he always worshiped the false god Baal. Just like his mother, he told the people they should not listen to Elijah. But Ahaziah was very, very wrong.

One day, the king had a bad accident. Ahaziah fell from the roof and was badly hurt. He ordered his servants to find the priests of Baal. "Find out if I'm going to die," he told them.

But on the way, these servants met Elijah. "Tell the king the Lord wants to know why he looks for answers from a false god like Baal. The Lord God knows what will happen to King Ahaziah. Tell him God says he will die from his injuries!"

When the servants heard this, they hurried back to the palace. They told the king what had happened. "What?" the king roared. "My mother told me about this Elijah. He caused a great deal of trouble for her and my father. Now he has bad news for me. I know one way of making sure he never bothers us again.

"You there," he pointed at an officer of the guard. "Take fifty men and capture Elijah."

The officer found Elijah praying on top of a hill. "Man of God, come with us!" he ordered.

Elijah called out, "If I am a man of God, then may fire fall from heaven and kill you!" Suddenly, fire rained down on the soldiers, killing them all.

The king sent another fifty men to take Elijah, but the same thing happened. When the third fifty men came to Elijah hill, the captain fell to his knees. "Please," he begged Elijah. "Please, have mercy on us."

An angel from God told Elijah, "Go with him and do not be afraid."

So Elijah listened and did as the angel told him. Once in the palace, Elijah told Ahaziah, "You should have trusted God. Why didn't you ask Him if you were going to get better? Why do you trust Baal more than the Lord? Why? Because you are very bad. You are even worse than your father. Yes, you are going to die!"

And it happened just as Elijah had said it would.

All his life Elijah fought the evil Jezebel, trying to lead the Israelites back to God. When Jezebel finally died, she was pushed from a balcony and fell to the ground. By the time people found her next to the palace, dogs had already eaten her up. It was a terrible ending for a terrible queen.

Elijah taught Elisha everything he knew. They were like father and son. When Elijah was very, very old, he and Elisha walked into the desert together.

Elijah told Elisha, "You stay here. I must go away."

"But I will never leave you," young Elisha said. He was sad because he knew that the Lord was going to take Elijah away Some prophets followed the men, but Elisha and Elijah left them behind when they reached the River Jordan. There, Elijah took off his cloak and hit the water. The river split in two and the men crossed the nver on dry ground.

Once on the other side a golden chariot of fire suddenly blazed through the sky! Fiery horses pulled it down from heaven. Elijah climbed into the chariot and was taken away from Elisha.

"My father! My father! Oh, now you are goner Elisha cried out as the fiery whirlwind carried Elijah, the prophet of fire up to heaven to be with God Elijah stayed in heaven for many, many years. Then, during the time that Jesus walked the earth, Elijah came back from heaven to talk with Jesus. The message Elijah preached all his life was true then, and is still true today. No one or nothing should be more important to God's people than praying to the one true Lord God.

You can find the story of Elijah in the Old Testament
from the book of First Kings, chapter 16 to the book of Second Kings, chapter 2.

ESTHER

A Woman Who Was as Courageous as She Was Beautiful

By Marlee Alex

Illustrated by Tiziana Gironi

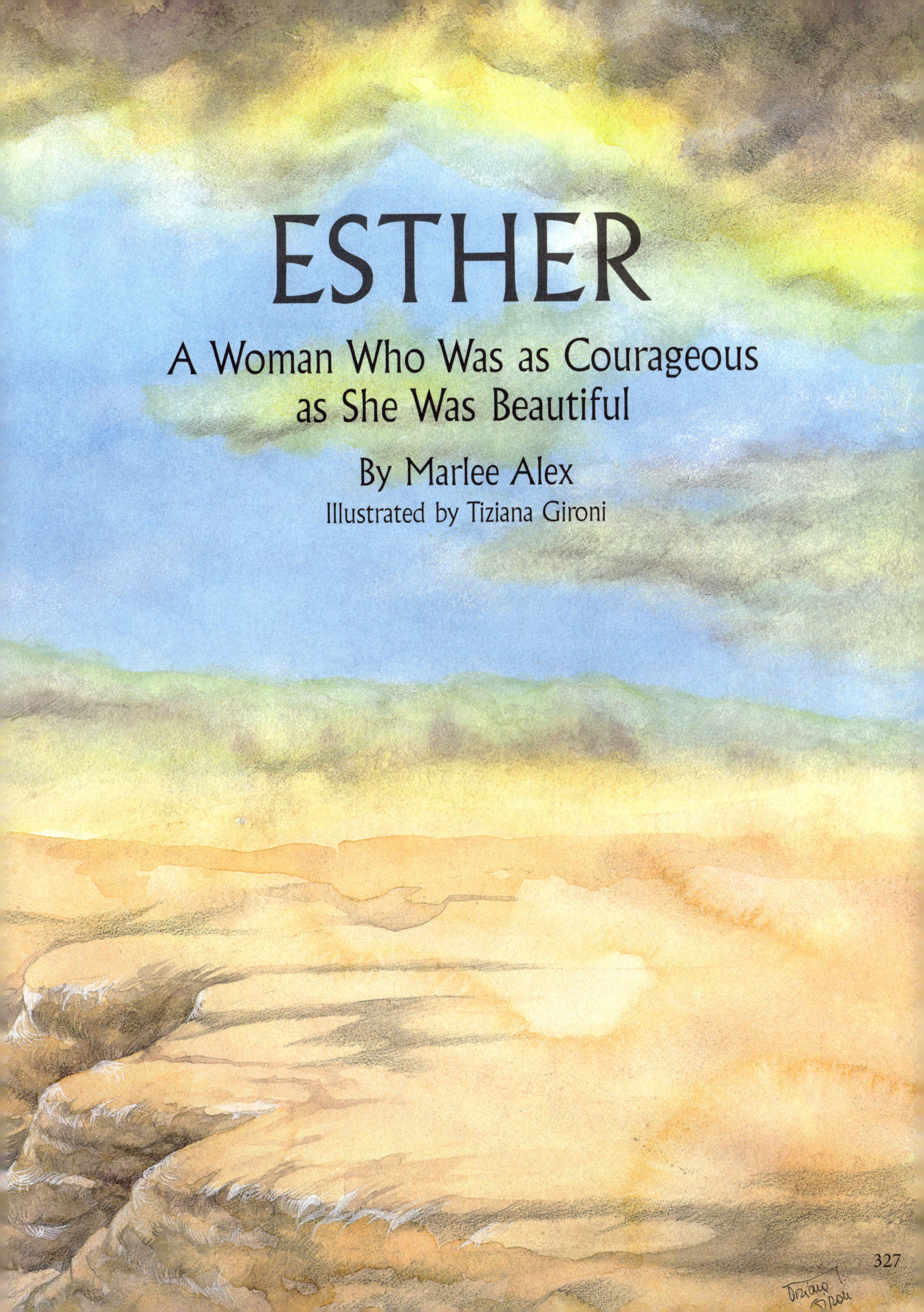

ESTHER

A Woman Who Was as Courageous as She Was Beautiful

By Marlee Alex

Illustrated by Tiziana Gironi

The marble columns in the courtyard gleamed in the sunlight. It was high noon on the seventh day of the feast. The king's guests were half-drunk already. Some of them moved clumsily over the mosaic floors, floors that were magnificent even for the king of the vast Persian empire. Jewels and pearls sparkled among the other colored stones under their feet. Then King Ahasuerus swung his heavy golden wine goblet in the air and commanded his servants to fetch his wife, Queen Vashti.

The princes, noblemen and officers who were guests at the feast shouted. "Yes, bring the queen," they exclaimed as they pulled away the purple linen drapes that shut off the inside of the palace. "She is more beautiful than all the other royal treasures put together!"

The servants hurried to the banquet room where the queen was entertaining the ladies. But they returned without her.

"What?" exclaimed King Ahasuerus.

"The queen refuses to come?"

The king was embarrassed in front of his guests. And he was angry. He, the most powerful man in an empire that stretched from India to Ethiopia, was a man whom all others were eager to please. He was accustomed to having his every wish instantly fulfilled. Yet, now his own wife ignored him.

He gathered the princes and noblemen around him "What should I do about this insulting behavior of the queen?" he asked.

"Well, you'll have to do something about it, Ahasuerus," the men complained "If your wife disobeys you, then our wives are likely to start treating us in the same way. Soon, women all over the empire will begin to nag their husbands."

"Send her away!" insisted one of the princes "And tell everyone why you are doing it."

So the king sent a decree throughout the empire, translated into each language of each province. It stated that every man must take charge of his household in an orderly manner and must not allow his wife to disobey. Of course, the king knew that he had to set the example. So Queen Vashti was banished from the empire.

Not too many days passed, however, before King Ahasuerus was sorry about what he had done. He missed his wife In order to cheer him up, his noblemen suggested that a new queen be chosen. They proposed that a search be made far and wide, and that the prettiest maidens found in the empire be brought to the palace for one year. They were to be pampered like princesses, treated with the most expensive perfumes, facial creams, and make-up, and then presented

to the king one by one. When the king had seen all the young women, he could choose the one he liked best to be his queen.

King Ahasuerus was delighted with the idea. He felt certain that he could find a woman just as beautiful as his former queen, and one who would never make a fool of him. To ensure this, he would set up strict regulations about when she was allowed to see him, and about what was expected of her. And so, the king announced that a beauty contest was to be held at the palace.

There was a man named Mordecai living in the capital city, not far from the palace. He was a Jew, a descendant of the Israelites. In this man's home lived a young woman named Esther She was a cousin of Mordecai whom he had taken into his household when she was small and raised as his own daughter.

Esther's skin was smooth as silk, her complexion, a tawny olive. Her eyes were large and expressive, framed by a thick rim of dark lashes. "She qualifies for the beauty contest," said the king's men And she was the first one chosen.

Esther was a high-spirited young woman, but her zest was tempered by grace and kindness. She soon became a favorite of Hegai, the servant who was in charge of all the maidens. Esther was given the nicest room at the palace, and seven maids to wait upon her and to lavish her with beauty treatments. She was given the first choice of exotic fruits and of luxurious clothes.

In spite of this, her cousin Mordecai was worried about her. He had no choice but to let her go, but he gave her instructions not to reveal that she was Jewish. Every day he took a walk past the garden fence near her window. At those times he was comforted by her smile and the happy expression on her face.

At last the day arrived when Esther was to meet the king. Hegai asked if she would like to choose for herself the clothes she wished to wear. "And choose some things from among this jewelry," he offered, handing her an ornately handcarved wooden box. The box was edged by rows of emeralds and rubies.

Esther carefully set the box down on her dresser and lifted its heavy lid. The contents of the box stunned her. It was full of necklaces, rings, brooches, bracelets, pearls to drape in the hair, and jeweled combs to set it with. Esther had never seen anything so magnificent. Her fingers caressed the sparkling jewels as she turned to Hegai.

"I am from an ordinary family," she replied "Why should I pretend to be rich and important? If I am to wear any of this, then you must choose it for me."

Hegai drew out a single strand of glistening pearls and hung it around her neck. Then he chose for her a silk dress without trim. It fit her perfectly. Hegai knew that the simplest clothing would make the king notice Esther's natural beauty, the kind of beauty which shines from the inside out.

As Esther passed through long corridors on her way to the king's apartment, the palace servants stopped what they were doing to admire her When the king set eyes on her, he knew he did not need to look further for his queen. He declared an official holiday throughout the empire, ordered a great feast at the palace and sent gifts to each province to celebrate his marriage to Esther.

The days and years of EEsther's reign as queen passed quickly for her. During this time, her cousin Mordecai became an officer in the Imperial Guard just inside the palace gates. One day Mordecai overheard two of the other officers planning to kill the king. He told Esther about it, and she reported it. The king's life was saved, and Mordecai's name was recorded in the Imperial Record Book.

Not long afterward, the king appointed a new Chief of State whose name was Haman. Haman was proud. He wanted all servants and other officials to bow down whenever he passed by. Everyone was careful to do it, for Haman was a rough and cruel man That is, everyone bowed down to Haman except Mordecai.

"I am a Jew," Mordecai insisted. "As a Jew, I cannot bow down to anyone except God."

This made Haman mad. He wanted to have Mordecai hanged to death. But he decided to do something even worse. He decided to have all the Jewish people in the empire killed. And he decided to make a game of it by throwing a pair of dice to determine the exact day it should happen In this way he could spread terror and fear among them.

Haman told the king about his plan.

"There is a race of people who do not obey your laws," he argued. "These people should be destroyed. Otherwise all the people in the empire will begin to act the same way."

The king did not bother to ask for any details. "Do as you like," he said as he took off the ring that had his initials on it.
He gave the ring to Haman to use to seal the death order, for the king was used to giving Haman whatever the man wanted.
Haman marched out happily. He sealed the order with the king's ring, and sent it by running messengers to the governors of each province. The order commanded them to kill all Jews, young and old, including women and children, on a certain day at a certain time. Haman promised the governors that they would be remembered as heroes for doing this.

The Jewish people in the capital city were the first to hear the order. They began to panic. When Mordecai heard about it, he ran through the streets, straight to the palace gates, shouting and crying. Hour by hour the news spread, until Jews everywhere became sick with terror. They refused to eat, they tore their clothes, and sprinkled themselves with ashes as a way of protesting to God and the king.

Back at the palace, Queen Esther had not heard about the order to kill all Jews. No one, not even the king, had any idea that she was Jewish. She had been alone in her own apartment for more than thirty days. The king had not sent for her, and it was forbidden for her to even ask to see the king.

The days had been lonely for Esther. A sad feeling grew in her heart. It was as if the king had forgotten about her. She was afraid he was angry with her. The worry and the hurt made her imagine that he was planning to send her away just as he had Queen Vashti.

Esther was supposed to be protected from all political affairs. But one of her maids

reported that Mordecai was lying at the palace gates dressed in a robe of goat hair and covered by ashes Esther was horrified. She sent the maid out to talk to Mordecai.

Mordecai gave a copy of Haman's order to the maid, asking her to tell Esther about the tenor which had spread among the Jews. He sent this message to

Esther: "Go to the king and tell him that you are also Jewish Plead with him to save the lives of your people throughout his empire."

Esther began to tremble from head to foot when she received the message. She sat down and scribbled a note to Mordecai. "Everyone knows that the queen cannot speak with the king unless she has been asked. I could be put to death just for seeking permission to see him. I am afraid he is angry with me anyway."

But Mordecai begged in return, "Do you think that your life will be saved just because you are the queen? God can find someone else to help the Jews if you are afraid to speak up. But you and your family will be killed. Have faith, Esther! Perhaps God has made you queen for this very reason."

Esther sighed deeply and shuddered. The thought of coming before the king was scary enough, but to let him find out that his own wife was Jewish, and to ask him to reverse one of his own sealed commands was unthinkable. Her head drooped and tears began to pour from her eyes. No, she would never dare to do it.

Then, someone began to speak quietly to Esther's heart. The voice became stronger and more urgent. At last, she could not ignore it, nor could she argue with the message: "Perhaps God has made you queen for this very reason."

Esther lifted her head and felt her spirits rise with it. "Return to Mordecai," she whispered to her maid. "Tell him to gather all the Jews in the city. Ask them to pray and go without food for three days I will do the same Then, even though it is forbidden, I will go to the king. If I am to die for my people, the Jews, then let it be so."

Esther prayed continuously for three days just as she had promised. Then she rubbed sweet-smelling oils on her skin, put on her red gown and slowly made her way to the throne room where the king was sitting. She stopped just out of his sight and waited in the shadows. A dim lamp flickered against the wall. Her heart was pounding, but her dark eyes were steady and determined.

The king seemed to feel that she was there. The scent of her perfume filled the room. He turned his head slightly and saw her standing in the soft, shimmering light. She could never have imagined how lovely she looked. She was not aware of the grace with which she moved as she knelt before the king. Her beauty reawakened forgotten feelings in his heart.

The king lifted his golden scepter toward Esther. It was a sign that he welcomed her, a sign that she did not need to be afraid Esther stepped closer and touched the tip of his scepter with her fingers. A look of tenderness passed between them.

"What is it, Esther? I will give you anything you wish, even the half of my kingdom," offered King Ahasuerus.

Esther's heart was pounding again. She did not feel peaceful in her spirit. She hesitated, lowered her eyes, and quietly answered, "I wish for the pleasure of your company at dinner this afternoon, together with Haman, your Chief of State."

"Yes, we would love to come We will come as soon as we possibly cant" the king replied.

Later, when the three of them were sitting on their couches around the table, the king lifted his wine glass and said, "Come now, tell me, Esther. What is it you wish for me to give you? I will give you anything!"

The king's question once again made Esther feel uneasy. Something seemed to tell her that the time was not right to say what she had intended. Instead she answered, "I wish to enjoy the pleasure of your company here at my table again tomorrow. If you truly wish to make me happy, please come Then I will tell you."

The two men left the table that day feeling satisfied and happy with themselves, especially Haman. At home he bragged to his family and servants that he had been to dinner with the king and queen, and had been invited again for the next day.

"But that miserable Mordecai!" Haman exclaimed. "Again today he refused to bow before me when I left the palace gates It is humiliating!"

"He should be hanged immediately!" Haman's wife declared.

"Good ideal" replied Haman. He ordered a gallows built that very day and decided to ask permission of the king first thing the next morning.

However, that night the king woke up and could not fall asleep again. Wanting to put the time to good use, he began to read his official record books. At dawn, he was reading the part about the two officers of

the Imperial Guard who had planned to kill him but whose plan was reported in time by a man named Mordecai. "Has this Mordecai ever been rewarded?" he asked one of his aides at breakfast.

"No, but he still faithfully keeps watch at the palace gates."

Right then and there the king decided to do something to reward Mordecai. When Haman arrived for work that morning, King Ahasuerus met him at the door and asked, "Tell me, how should I reward a man who has won my favor?"

Haman thought to himself, "Who could have won the king's favor more than I?" So he answered, "Put your own royal robe on his shoulders and place a crown on his head Let him sit upon your own horse as one of your most noble princes leads him through the streets shouting, This is the way the king rewards those who win his favor.' "

"A marvelous suggestion!" answered the king with a broad smile. "Here, you take this robe and crown, fetch my horse and go throughout the city leading Mordecai, the Jew upon it. Take care that you shout as loudly as you can, 'This is the way the king rewards those who win his favor!' "

Haman looked at the king in shock. It would never do to let the king know that he had intended to have Mordecai hanged to death that very day. Instead, Haman forced a faint smile upon his lips and nodded to the king. "Y-y--yes, Your Majesty," he stuttered. And so Haman was forced to do what the king had ordered.

That afternoon Haman showed up as expected at the queen's apartment for dinner. This time when the king asked Esther why she had invited them, Esther replied, "If you truly love me, then save my life and the lives of my people throughout the empire. For there is a decree that all Jews are to be killed on the 28th day of February this year."

"Who would order such a cruel thing?"demanded the king angrily.

"This man Haman," Esther replied softly.

The face of Haman turned ash-white, and he fell at Queen Esther's knees begging for mercy. King Ahasuerus was overcome by surprise. He stormed out of the room, then returned suddenly. Finding Haman still clinging to the queen, he became furious. He demanded that Haman be hanged that very day.

Esther began to weep. Tears spilled like raindrops down her pale cheeks. The worry and fear, the struggle for courage, and the decision for faith were all behind her now, but had made her weak. The king looked down and once again held out his golden scepter to Esther. At that moment she knew that, together, they would find a way to save the lives of the Jewish people.

Haman was hanged upon the very gallows he had built for Mordecai. Mordecai became Chief of State in Haman's place. And from that day on, Esther grew in favor with the king and as an influence upon the affairs of the empire.

Esther found the courage to risk her life by putting her faith in God. She trusted his quiet voice and learned that his timing is always perfect.

You can find the story of Esther in the Old Testament
in the book of Esther.

DANIEL

Prisoner With a Promise

By Anne de Graaf

Illustrated by José Pérez Montero

DANIEL

Prisoner With a Promise

By Anne de Graaf

Illustrated by José Pérez Montero

Daniel took one last look. There was no going back Suddenly, a whip bit into his shoulder! Daniel cried out.

"You there," the soldier shouted in a strange language "Move along!"

Daniel had never heard the words before. He knew what the whip meant, though. He was a slave, taken pnsoner by the horrible Babylonian army. Daniel tned to rub the cuts. The rope around his hands would not let him He was tied to the boy in front.

The same rope bound a long string of boys like himself. They headed out of Jerusalem, toward Babylon. They would never see their home again.

Home. His father had died earlier that year in battle. Daniel thought about his mother. He had last seen her that morning when soldiers dragged her off to join the other women slaves. Daniel could still hear her screams. She had called for her only son as they took her away. "Daniel! My Daniell Remember the God of our fathers! Daniel!..." He would never see her again either.

Daniel watched the tears drop into the dust. He stumbled through smoke-filled streets. Walls and buildings crashed down around him Daniel heard nothing. He saw nothing. He had lost his freedom, his home and his mother all in one day.

"Daniel! Daniel!" His mother's words echoed through his thoughts. He looked up. The voice was real! Who was calling him? Then Daniel saw a man watching him from between the piles of rubble. The man nodded at Daniel.

Daniel gasped, "The prophet!" He was called Jeremiah. Daniel had heard that the Babylonian king offered Jeremiah a place at his court The prophet had said no. He would rather stay with his people in Jerusalem, a ruined city.

"Daniel!" The prophet called him again. Daniel strained to listen. Above the soldier's strange shouts he heard for the second time that day, "Remember the God of our fathers!"

Seeing the prophet helped Daniel think of something besides his loss. Daniel remembered the first time he ever heard Jeremiah. He had been a very small boy. There he had stood, holding both his parents' hands while listening to the strange man shout.

"Stop worshiping false gods! Stop hurting the poor! Stop caring so much about money and things! Come back to God!"

Most of the people had laughed, but not Daniel's parents. They were among a very few of the rich people in Jerusalem who believed the prophet. That evening they had prayed as a family for all the people who were hurting God.

Daniel's parents taught him to give to the poor. He was brought up worshiping the one God. This was the God of their fathers, and their fathers before them. They had taught him the religious laws. Daniel had grown up with the love of God in his heart.

In the years to come Daniel would often hear Jeremiah warning the people, "The

Lord wants to forgive you! Stop living such bad lives. You're only bringing disaster upon yourselves!"

And now disaster had struck. Jerusalem lay in ruins. All the rich and powerful people had thought they no longer needed God. Now the Babylonians were leading them off as captives to a faraway land.

A year-and-a-half ago the Babylonian army had surrounded Jerusalem. They stopped all food from entering the city. Month after long month the people had bravely gone with less and less food The Babylonians had starved the people into giving up.

Daniel could no longer remember his last full meal It did not matter. Even when all they had was some watery soup, his mother had taught him to remember God and give thanks.

Now Daniel dragged his feet, tired and weak from the hunger and fear. Daniel said out loud to himself, "Yes, I will remember. No matter what, I will remember God. I have to."

When Daniel spoke, the boy in front turned his head. "What did you say?"

Daniel looked up in surprise. The boy had been stumbling along, looking half dead. "I said, no matter what they do to me, I won't forget God " He paused, then added, "You shouldn't either."

The boy's headed bobbed up and down. "You're right No matter where they take us, we can't forget who we are."

The boy behind Daniel pulled on his rope. "You up there," he called. "I heard what you said. Even if they never let us go home again, I'm never going to forget where I came from."

Daniel looked from one boy, back to the other. He had seen them before, but did not know them well. Their families, like his, had believed in the one God. A shiver ran up his back. He wondered, "Has God put the three of us together for a reason?"

"You there," he tugged at the rope in front of him. "And you, behind me, listen. The three of us are brothers. I don't care what happens to us We must swear never to for-

get who our God is. He'll stay with us wherever we go. Do you promise?"

"I swear it," the boy in front said.

"Yes, I swear," the boy behind Daniel said. "We're sons of God's chosen people. I'll never forget that."

"Good," Daniel smiled for the first time all day. " Now tell me your names."

And so began a very special friendship between Daniel, Hananiah and Mishael. When the guards weren't watching, the boys whispered messages back and forth. They remained tied to each other for the rest of the long trip east. Day and night they walked through the desert, depending on when it was coolest.

They shared their food and prayed for each other. They told stories After some time they even spoke about their families and homes. Just having someone to talk with somehow helped the pain to lessen. It did not go away, though. All three boys had lost too much for the hurt to heal completely. Only God could make that happen.

Somewhere in the desert, Daniel left his childhood behind. The long weeks of walking, the soldiers' whips, the pain of loss, it crushed the boy out of Daniel. He became a man at the age of thirteen.

The day finally came when the army and its prisoners arrived at Babylon This was the largest and richest city of its time. Great temples and palaces spread out for miles around. Daniel had never seen such wealth.

He and his friends were taken to the great palace of Nebuchadnezzar, king of Babylon He was the most powerful man on earth. Daniel walked down marble hallways. Fountains and gardens appeared around every corner. Finally he arrived in a huge hall. He saw hundreds of boys and young men just like himself, all taken prisoner and brought there by the Babylonians.

A very important man who worked for the king was interviewing each of the boys. He asked them questions about their families, schooling and health.

When it was Daniel's turn, Daniel was surprised to hear this man speak his own language. "I am Ashpenaz," he said. "I want you to tell me about yourself."

Daniel answered all the man's questions. What he did not know, was that Ashpenaz was helping the king. Nebuchadnezzar wanted all the smartest boys who came from the best of families to go to a special school If they did well they could someday work in the king's court. That would be much better than working as a slave in the fields, or hauling bricks at the building sites.

Soon Daniel was called back This time to a different hall. There he heard he had been chosen for the special school. It was one chance in a thousand. "Thank you, God. You are with me, even here."

Daniel looked around to see who his classmates would be. His heart jumped. There were Hananiah and Mishael! He had not seen them since they all had arrived in Babylon.

"Brothers! There you are! Now look at us, going back to school together!"

The three young men hugged each other. Knotted ropes no longer tied them together. Now it was their faith in God which bound them for life.

It did not take long for the three young men to be joined by a fourth Young Azariah had overheard Daniel and his friends talking about their promise to God. He, too, felt in his heart the need to worship God, especially there, in that far-away land. Daniel, Hananiah and Mishael were only too glad to welcome Azariah. Together they would continue to follow the religious laws of their people.

They did not have long to wait for the first test. The king had ordered Ashpenaz to spend three years teaching his young men the Babylonian language and culture. Not only that, Ashpenaz was supposed to make sure the boys all grew into tall, strong young men.

For that the king had ordered him to feed the boys only the best food and drink. The first time such a meal was brought to Daniel, though, he moaned.
"Mishael," he whispered to his friend. "Look at this. You know how long it has been since any of us ate a good meal. But this is pork And this meat here still has the blood in it. We're not allowed to eat this."

Daniel made up his mind then and there. "No matter what, I won't forget what my parents taught me. Eating this food is against God's own Law. I can't drink this wine, either."

Daniel went to Ashpenaz. "Please sir, my friends and I cannot eat this food. A long time ago our God gave my people a list of rules. I cannot break those rules, even if I no longer live in my homeland."

Ashpenaz looked at the tall young man. He had noticed Daniel before. He was a natural leader The other boys went to him with their problems. He seemed wise beyond his years. Ashpenaz could read the stubborn look in Daniel's brown eyes. The boy meant what he said.

Ashpenaz sadly shook his head at Daniel. He hated to say no to the boy, but had no choice. "I'm afraid of my lord, the king. He is the one who has said you must eat this food. If you do not eat it, he will notice you looking thinner than the rest. Once he found out I had not followed his orders, I would surely be killed."

So Daniel and his friends asked God to show them what they should do. They each knew that if they gave in and failed this first test, it would become that much easier to forget the God of their fathers in the years to come. Their promise would mean nothing.

Then the Lord gave the boys an idea. Daniel went to the cook. "Please, sir, just test us for ten days. Feed us nothing but vegetables and water See for yourself if we don't look healthier than the others when the ten days are up."

A few of the other boys laughed at Daniel and his friends. They were different. "Why can't you just eat what everyone else does? Isn't it good enough for you?" they jeered.

Daniel and his friends knew they were different. That was all right. It was the choice they made when they promised to remember God.

Sure enough. When the ten days were up, Daniel and his friends had grown stronger and fatter than the boys eating the king's finest cooking Now no one teased them. They were different all right, they were healthier than the rest.

Daniel, Hananiah, Mishael and Azariah ate what they pleased for the rest of heir time at the king's school.

God blessed the young men with shining health They could run faster than any of the others They grew clever and wise in every subject. Daniel even knew how to tell people what their dreams meant.

But the young men knew these were all gifts from God. Daily they remembered God and thanked Him. They said the prayers their parents had taught them.

At the end of the three years, Ashpenaz brought each boy before the king. Nebuchadnezzar himself tested the young men to see how much they had learned.

When it was Daniel's turn, the king could hardly believe his eyes and ears. Daniel stood tall and sure of himself. He spoke the language as if he had grown up in Babylon. No one would have guessed this was the same boy who could not understand a soldier who was whipping him.

Of all the students, Daniel and his three friends were the smartest of all. The king told Ashpenaz, "Why, they are ten times brighter than all the magicians in my kingdom. I want them to work for me I need wise men like them to help me run my kingdom."

So the great palace of Nebuchadnezzar became Daniel's place of work. He would no longer have to fear soldiers' whips Daniel had become one of the most honored men in the kingdom. This did not come without a price, though.

Not long after Daniel began working for the king, he faced yet another test. The king was having bad dreams. Night after night he woke up in a cold sweat.

Finally King Nebuchadnezzar called his magicians. "I want you to tell me what this bad dream means. It makes me so worried, I can't even sleep anymore."

"Great king, tell us your dream and we will tell you what it means!" the magicians said.

But the king was clever. He thought to himself, "How do I know they won't just make something up? I must know the truth."

King Nebuchadnezzar said, "I meant what I said. Tell me what the dream was. Then tell me what it meant. I know you have been trying to be crafty. So tell me now what I saw in my dream."

"We can't do that. No one can do that. No king has ever asked that of his magicians before. How can we possibly know what your dream was?"

At this, the king shook his fist in rage. "Kill them!" he ordered his guards. "Kill them all All the magicians and wise men, they are nothing but liars. I want them all dead, every single one of them!"

Daniel heard loud knocking and hurried downstairs to answer the door. The captain of the king's guard stood there, holding his sword.

"Yes, Arioch. How can I help you?" Daniel smiled at the soldier. He knew him well.

"Daniel, I'm afraid I've come to arrest you. I. . . I have orders to kill you." Daniel's eyes grew very round, but he said nothing.

"The king has ordered us to kill all magicians and wise men That means you and your friends."

"But why? I don't understand. . . ." Daniel motioned for the captain to come in. Daniel closed the door behind him. Once inside, Arioch put down his sword. Here no one would see him disobeying orders. Arioch told the story of the king's dream to Daniel.

Daniel nodded. "Arioch, wait. Please let me go to the king and speak with him about this."

"Would you, Daniel? Maybe you can even help him." Daniel said nothing, but left for the king right away.

Once at the palace he asked the king to please give him a little more time. "I did not know about your problem earlier. With more time I may be able to tell you what you want to know." The king nodded. He was still too furious to speak.

Daniel ran to his friends' homes. "Hurry! It's a matter of life and death. You must pray with me tonight!" He told them what had happened The four dropped everything. They asked God to please save them. "Please show us the king's dream." All night they pleaded with God.

Then, in a night vision, Daniel saw the dream. Daniel blessed God, "You are light. You, 0 God of my fathers have given me wisdom and power. Thank You!"

Daniel hurried to Arioch. "Stop! Don't kill any of the wise men! I know the king's dream! Take me to him before anyone gets hurt over this! Hurry!" Arioch was only too glad to do as Daniel asked.

“O king, I have found one of the foreigners. He can tell you what the dream means!”

The king narrowed his eyes at Daniel. “How can you possibly know what I dreamed, let alone what it means?” This king was no fool.

Daniel took a deep breath. “You are right. No wise man or magician can read the king’s mind. But there is a God in heaven who knows your thoughts. Your dreams were about times still to come.

“As for me,” Daniel continued, “I only know these things because the God of my fathers has shown me. He wants you to know what will happen in the future.”

The king leaned forward and thought to himself, “This young man always did make good sense. Yet, I wonder if he can tell me what I dreamed.”

Daniel closed his eyes “In your dream you saw a great statue. Its different parts were made of gold, silver, bronze, iron and clay. As you watched, the feet, legs and other parts of the body were broken off and crushed by a stone. Then that stone became a great mountain.

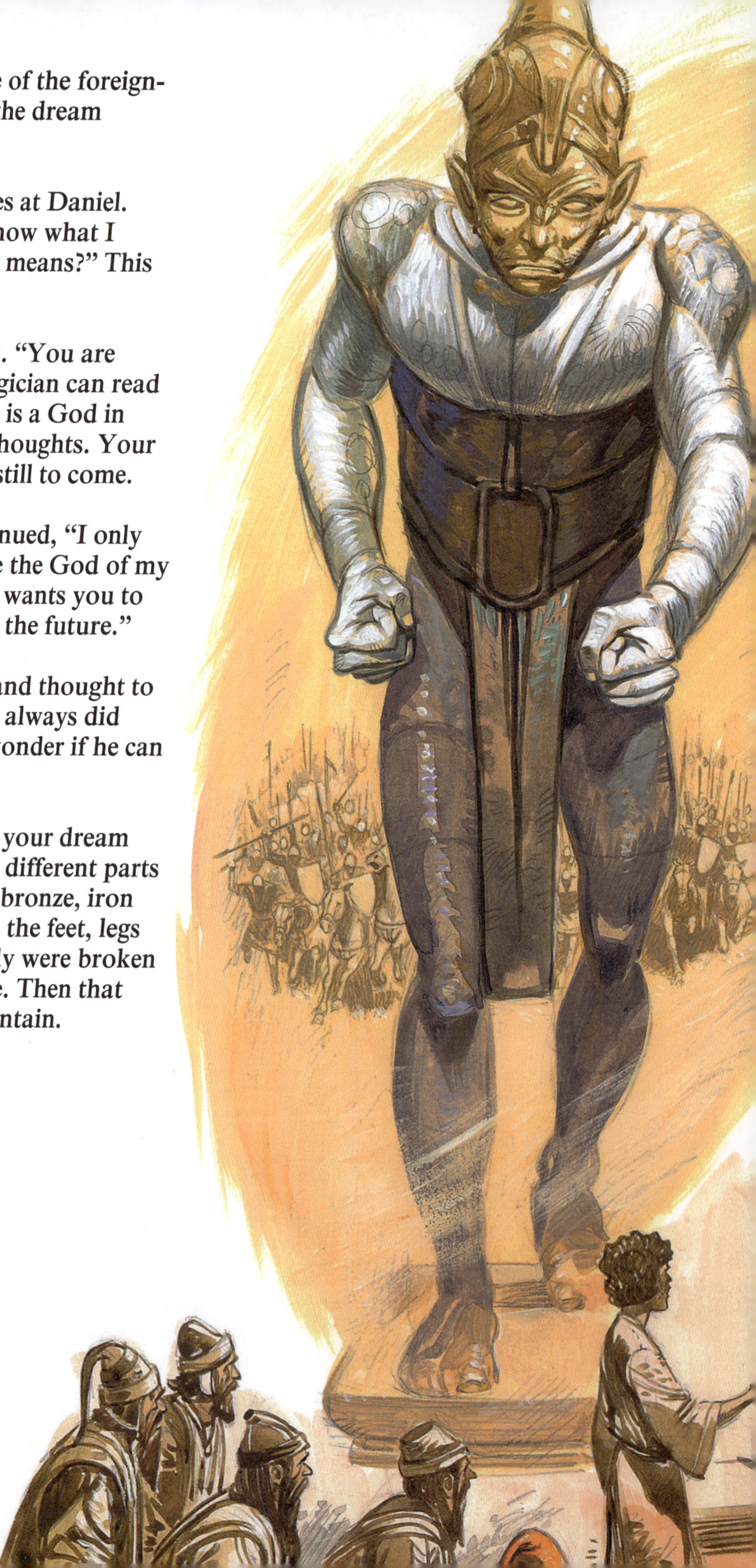

"Each of the parts of the statue are nations who will rule the world in the days to come. You, 0 king, are the head of gold. In the end, though, all the kingdoms will be destroyed and a kingdom of God will rule over all the earth."

Daniel looked at the king. He had prayed all night and had not stopped since he entered the throne room If what he had said was the wrong answer, the king would surely order him to be killed Daniel waited.

The king had stopped looking at Daniel Now, very slowly, he stood Arioch and all the guards and servants held their breath. King Nebuchadnezzar took a step toward Daniel Then, suddenly, he knelt down on the ground!

"Surely, your God is a Lord of kings, the God of gods, that He could show you this secret of mine." The king then gave Daniel many beautiful gifts. He put him in charge of all the wise men and made him ruler over Babylon.

Daniel asked one thing only He wanted his three friends, his prayer partners, to help him rule.

This would not be the last time that God showed Daniel what dreams meant. Daniel was wise and clever like no other man in the kingdom. He and his friends were different than the rest of the magicians. They prayed only to the God of their fathers and never worshiped any of the Babylonian gods. God blessed them for this, so they were able to solve many deep and dark mysteries.

Many years after this first test of Daniel's skill, King Nebuchadnezzar had another terrible dream. Again he called Daniel in to tell him what it meant.

This time, though, Daniel was so appalled at what the Lord showed him, he could hardly speak.

"Tell me what you know," the king asked when he saw Daniel's face.

"I wish it were about your enemies, but your dream is about yourself. There will come a day when you no longer think of your kingdom as a gift from God. You will become proud of your power. Then God will strike you down and you will become like an animal in the fields! You will even eat grass! But after a time God will give you another chance. Then you will know in your heart that God, not man, has the power to make.. . and break all kings and rulers."

Everything happened just as Daniel predicted. Exactly a year later, King Nebuchadnezzar was walking on the palace roof, thinking about how wonderful he was All at once, his mind became very sick. No one could help the king, so he lived outside like an animal. His hair grew long and his fingernails looked like birds' claws.

But at the end of that period, the king looked up at the sky and remembered who he was. Even more important, he remembered who God was.

Daniel watched all this happening. Years later Daniel heard that the great King Nebuchadnezzar had finally died. He knew the king's last years had been his best because he gave God the glory.

In the years to come, Daniel would continue to serve the courts of different kings. He was still a prisoner, but he was also their wise man, counselor and interpreter of dreams. During this time, Daniel became an old man. Never once did he turn his back on God.

As the years went by, the kings of Babylon became weaker and weaker. There was never another king as great as Nebuchadnezzar. The last king of Babylon was a man named Belteshazzar. He was a very proud man and did whatever he pleased.

One night, King Belteshazzar was throwing a wild party. He decided he was as great as any god. "I should be able to eat off plates and drink from cups which have been used by gods," he bragged to his guests. So Belteshazzar called for the gold and silver plates and cups which Nebuchadnezzar had taken from the temple in Jerusalem.

These were plates and cups the temple priests had used when offering sacrifices to God. This was very, very wrong of Belteshazzar. "Let's worship the gods of gold and silver!" the king shouted to his guests.

Now Belteshazzar had gone too far. All at once, a horrible hand came out of nowhere and began writing on the wall! The huge fingers wrote three words on the wall, then it disappeared. The king's face grew pale. He suddenly felt like he should sit down. His knees knocked together so badly, all his guests could hear his fear.

"Get me the magicians," the king gasped.

"I need to know what those words mean." When the magicians and wizards arrived, though, nobody could help the king.

The magicians all hummed and hawed. "Should we make something up?" they whispered to each other.

We had better not. Remember how Nebuchadnezzar felt about that."

Finally, a very, very old woman entered the hall. She was the queen mother of Nebuchadnezzar. "0 king, there's no need to look so pale. My son knew a wise and wonderful man. He is a foreigner, taken from Jerusalem as a young boy. I am sure he can read this writing on the wall for you."

Daniel looked around the great hall. He did not like what he saw. The king's food and drink and wild parties, all went very much against what Daniel believed. But the worst sin of all was that of pride. Daniel had seen how pride could bring a man down when Nebuchadnezzar lost his mind.

Now Daniel's eyes fell on the gold and silver plates from his temple in Jerusalem. He gasped! How dare the king? Daniel remembered the last time he had seen those treasures. He had been a boy, worshiping with his parents. When they dragged him away from his home, so many, many years ago, he had sworn never to forget what that meant.

Daniel thought to himself, "I see that this king is very, very proud. He even thinks he should use the plates and cups of God's own temple."

Then Daniel saw the writing on the wall. The Lord made very clear to him what was happening. Daniel turned to the king. He shook his head. "Belteshazzar, I must tell you a story before I read the writing on the wall. It is a story you

have already heard, but chosen to forget."

Daniel told the king about Nebuchadnezzar and how mighty he had been. He told about Nebuchadnezzar's own pride, and how sick his mind became until he realized it was God who gives power and glory.

"Yet, you, Belteshazzar, have not humbled your heart, even though you knew all this You and your wives and guests have been drinking wine from cups which were offered to God. You have praised the gods of silver and gold, wood and stone. You honor all of them but the one God who rules over life and death. This hand was sent from Him.

"King Belteshazzar, the words on your wall say your kingdom will be taken away from you. You have not measured up. You have brought on the end of this Babylonian kingdom. Now it will be split between the Persians and Medes."

That very night it happened just as Daniel had said it would. King Belteshazzar was killed in his bed! A new king, Darius the Mede, came to power.

When King Darius took over Babylon, he chose three men to help him run the kingdom. One was Daniel It did not take long for Darius to see that Daniel was an old man of amazing gifts. 'Daniel could easily rule my kingdom all by himself. He's just the man I've been looking for," Darius said.

The other wizards, magicians and wise men did not like this at all! "Daniel in charge of everything?" they grumbled to each other. "Why, he's nothing but an old slave, some foreigner who doesn't even eat like we do! He's different than us!"

And that is when Daniel's enemies had an idea. "Let's use his differences to get rid of him once and for all," they plotted. These men went to the king with their plan.

"Hail, King Darius! As your wise men, we have decided it would be wise for you to sign an order lasting a month which tells everyone in the kingdom not to pray to any other gods but your majesty. If they don't, they should be thrown to the lions."

King Darius stroked his beard. "Yes, Pm sure the gods wouldn't mind taking a month's holiday." So he signed the order.

When Daniel heard the news, it changed nothing. All his life, Daniel had prayed to his God. Upstairs in Daniel's house there was a room where he prayed every day, sometimes all day.

The windows in that room looked toward Jerusalem, so very far away. Daniel had often gazed out those windows, remembering his home and family, both so far away. His God, though, had always stood by Daniel's side.

Daniel knew his enemies were waiting down on the street. They would sneak upstairs and catch him breaking the new law. It made no difference. Daniel looked out his favorite windows. Then he knelt to pray and give thanks to his God, the God of his fathers. In his heart he knew, this would be the most difficult test he had faced so far.

The king's advisors grabbed Daniel and dragged him to the palace. "Here he is! This is the man who broke your new law. We saw him ourselves. He was kneeling down and raying to another God. Now he must be thrown to the lions, just as you said."

King Darius groaned. "Not Daniel." Then he looked at the crafty men who had trapped him. "I. . .I will not let this happen."

"You must. It's the law. At sunset, we will throw him to the lions!"

All day long King Darius tried to think of a way to free Daniel. When the sun went down, though, he chose to do nothing. The other wise men had known Darius would never dare go against his own law.

As Daniel fell into the pit full of lions, the king called after him, "Have courage Daniel! Your God will stand by you!" The king knew too well that wild lions, hungry for meat, could tear a weak old man like Daniel to pieces. But would they?

All night long the king stayed awake worrying. He ate nothing. At first light, he rushed to the lions' den. "Daniell Oh Daniel, please be all right! Has your God saved you?"

A voice answered from deep inside the pit. "Long live the king! Yes! My God sent an angel who shut the lions' mouths! He knew I had done nothing wrong. You knew that, too."
King Darius was so excited, he jumped up and down. "Hurry," he ordered a guard. "Roll away the rock and help the poor man out of that place."

When Daniel was pulled out of the lions' den, there was not even one scratch on him! The king gave Daniel a big hug. Then he ordered the guards to arrest the men who had trapped Daniel.

"Throw them to the lions! And let's hope the poor animals don't get too sick."

Daniel went on to serve King Darius, always judging fairly. He helped to rule the kingdom with wisdom and justice.

All during his life the Lord showed Daniel many strange and wonderful visions. These were about the times to come. Some of the dreams Daniel had have already come true.

Perhaps the greatest of these thought pictures was about a time which is still part of our own future. When that time comes, all the people who have chosen to believe in God will shine like so many bright stars. These people will light the way forever and ever.

When Daniel died, he went to heaven. Just before his death, he prayed to God for his people. He knew their time in Babylon was almost over. Soon there would come a king who would let them all go back home.

Daniel's was the prayer of a lifetime, a prayer which had always made him different. With this prayer he hoped his people would never have to be dragged off again as prisoners to a strange land. "May we always turn to God. May we always remember the God of our fathers."

You can find the story of Daniel in the Old Testament
in the book of Daniel.

MARY

An Ordinary Woman with a Special Calling

By Marlee Alex

Illustrated by Ruth Imhoff

MARY

An Ordinary Woman with a Special Calling

By Marlee Alex

Illustrated by Ruth Imhoff

"Hello, Mary! God loves you," said a quiet voice.

Mary opened her sleepy eyes and looked up toward the open window. Light flooded her small bedchamber.

"God will give the world a wonderful Gift through you."

Mary heard, but could not see anyone. The light penetrating her room was brighter than the usual morning sun. It frightened her. But Mary admitted to herself, "It's not every day someone wakes me, saying something this exciting." So Mary waited and kept her eyes on the river of light.

As she watched, Mary realized it was a shining angel. It was the angel Gabriel. "Don't be afraid, Mary," Gabriel said. "God wants to show the world that He loves and cares for everyone. Your life is part of His plan."

Mary stared at the angel.

Gabriel continued, "God has chosen you to be the mother of His own Son. This time next year you will give birth to a baby boy. Name Him Jesus, because Jesus means 'savior.' Jesus will save people from the suffering and death caused by sin He will teach people how to enter the kingdom of God, a kingdom that will never end."

Mary rose up off her bed. "But I am so young!" she exclaimed. "I am not even married yet. I have never lived with a man. How can I have a baby?"

"It will happen in a way that has never happened before, and will never happen again," Gabriel assured Mary. "The Baby will be conceived by the power of God's Holy Spirit. He will be the Son of God Himself.

"And by the way," Gabriel added, "did you know that Elizabeth and Zacharias, your mother's relatives, are also going to have a baby?"

"But Elizabeth is too old to become pregnant," Mary protested.

"Yet, it is true!" exclaimed Gabriel. "She is already pregnant. God makes things possible that no one would dare to imagine!"

Mary's face lit up with joy. "I am really just a girl, the most ordinary girl in Nazareth. But I have always loved God and longed to be used by Him. I will do whatever He says. I do hope what you are saying is true."

Several days passed. Then Mary packed some clothes and started out over the hills of Galilee towards Judea where Elizabeth, her mother's cousin, lived. Elizabeth was much older than Mary As a little girl, Mary had often climbed up on her lap and listened to stories about the children of Israel and God s promise of a great king and savior It was Elizabeth who had been the source of inspiration in Mary's life and who had taught her to love God. Although Mary was eager to talk to Elizabeth about this amazing thing that was supposed to happen to her, she dared not tell Joseph about it.

Joseph was the man Mary would soon marry. The wedding festivities had been planned for months. Mary wondered as she skipped down the narrow roads of Galilee," Will Joseph believe I talked to an angel?What will he think when he finds out I am going to have a baby? Will he understand that it is God's own Child? The questions and worries flowed endlessly through Mary's mind as she hiked over the rocky hills of Judea. "Perhaps serving God is not going to be as simple as I dreamed it would,"she thought to herself.

At last Mary climbed the stone steps leading to Elizabeth's house. "Hello!" she called out. "Is anyone home? Elizabeth, it's me, Mary!"

Elizabeth was just inside the door. At the sound of Mary's voice, she felt her own unborn baby leap in her womb. Elizabeth was filled with the Holy Spirit. She began to exclaim happily as she flew down the steps, "Mary! What a blessing you bring with you, for you have been chosen by God above all other women. And the Child you will bear will be God's greatest Gift to the world. Mary, what an honor to have you visit me At the sound of your voice even my baby jumped for joy. For you believe God will do whatever He promises!"

Mary threw her arms around Elizabeth. "How can it be you know these things already?" she asked.

Mary's heart was filled with awe. "How happy I am in God, my Savior," she exclaimed. "How wonderful He is to look down and notice me. Surely, no one has ever known such joy. God has done great things for me! His love never ends; it is there for anyone who trusts Him."

Mary felt as if someone beyond herself were pouring these words of praise through her lips and saturating her heart with peace and joy. She lifted her hands toward the heavens and began to sing. "The arm of God is strong. He scatters all who think they are important. He takes power away from lungs and princes, but gives success to those who are humble. He fills the empty-hearted, but empties the hearts of those who think they have everything. Just look how He has helped Israel! He has never forgotten to show them mercy. He promised He would always love them."

Mary stayed with Elizabeth for about three months. The two women shared God's promises, and prayed together about the future. They spun wool, dyed it, and wove pretty baby blankets. They talked endlessly about what it would be like to raise little boys. They laughed, thinking forward to the time when the two boys could romp and play together.

Then Mary returned to Nazareth her womb began to grow round like Elizabeth's Mary knew it would soon be obvious to her family and friends that she was expecting a baby. It was time to talk to Joseph about it.

Mary wandered slowly through the narrow streets of Nazareth to Joseph's carpenter shop. He would be working this time of day. As she stepped out of the sunny street into the cool shadow of the workshop, Mary felt hopeful Joseph would understand. "Joseph," she said softly, "do you remember that the prophet Isaiah promised a son born in Israel who would be called the Prince of Peace?"

Then Mary told Joseph the angel Gabriel had come to her saying she was to be the mother of this Prince, God's Son. She told about her visit with Elizabeth. "Elizabeth already knew about this Child before I told her anything. She confirmed the words of the angel," Mary explained.

Joseph looked skeptical and angry, but he didn't say anything for a long time. Finally he answered, "Mary, I love you and want to trust you. But your story is unbelievable. I know God has promised a savior to Israel. But how can you expect me to believe this savior will come through an ordinary young woman like you? Don't tell me lies, Mary If you are going to have a baby, and I am not the baby's father, then we can never be married. I am disappointed and sorry, but I don't want to shame you. I will not tell anyone else about this. We'll break our engagement quietly."

Mary could not convince Joseph she was telling the truth. She left him alone and went home. "Joseph will never want to see me again," she thought sadly.

Day after day passed. Night after night Joseph lay awake, tossing and turning on his bed He could not get Mary out of his mind. One night when he was half-asleep and half-awake he thought he dreamed someone was standing beside his bed. But Joseph wasn't dreaming. It was an angel.

The angel whispered, "Joseph, Joseph! Go ahead and make Mary your wife, for what she has told you is true. The child she carries in her womb is God's own Child, conceived by the Holy Spirit. It will be a baby boy. Name Him Jesus, for He will save His people from their sin. He is the One God spoke of through His prophets, long ago."

Joseph could not sleep at all the rest of the night. The next morning he hurried down the hillside to the house where Mary lived. Taking her by surprise, he pleaded, "Forgive me, Mary. Last night an angel appeared to me in a dream and assured me everything you said was true. The angel said we should go ahead and be married while you wait for the birth of Jesus I praise God for your faith, Mary."

So Joseph and Mary were married as planned. Mary began to make a cozy home for Joseph and the baby. Eventually, the time grew close for her baby to be born. Mary was nervous and excited. She wanted everything to be ready and just right. Then something happened to upset her plans.

The Roman Emperor, Caesar Augustus, decided to find out exactly how many people were under his authority. He wanted to brag about it to his friends. He ordered everyone in his empire to make a trip to the birthplace of their grandparents in order to be counted and classified.

"We'll have to go to Bethlehem," Joseph told Mary. "Bethlehem is the home town of my ancestor, King David. You are to be counted as a member of my family, Mary."

"But Bethlehem is so far away!" Mary exclaimed. "The baby is due to be born any day now. What if he is born along the way, so far from home?"

"The emperor has ordered it, Mary," Joseph sighed. "No one can be excused from the trip."

Mary's womb was large and heavy now. Although the trip would be difficult, causing her and Joseph to travel slowly and carefully, they decided to trust God. "Perhaps this trip is part of God's plan," Mary pondered. "Surely, He will protect us and the baby."

The way was long and the roads were very crowded, but at last Joseph and Mary reached Bethlehem, a small village surrounded by fields and meadows. It was the home of shepherds and farmers, people living a quiet life.

Mary was exhausted from the journey. She felt a twmge of pain as she sat down to rest in the shade. Joseph set out to look for a place to stay. "Don't worry, Mary. I'll find a nice, comfortable room and a warm, clean bed for you," he said.

When Joseph returned, he looked angry and upset. “Mary, there are no more rooms available at the village inn. I’ve looked everywhere possible. But the innkeeper said there is fresh hay in the stable. He agreed we could sleep there tonight, and tomorrow I’ll look for a better place.”

“Oh, Joseph,” Mary cried. “I think the baby will be born tonight! We can’t stay in a stable!”

“Mary, people are already bedding down under the trees,” Joseph explained. “At least we can be alone if we stay in the stable. And the animals will keep it warm. We decided to trust God, remember? That means right now, even though it seems more difficult than ever.”

Mary’s face was contosted in disappointment and worry. The twinges of pain had given way to strong squeezing contrac-

tions in her womb. She knew she had no choice but to let God have control over her feelings and her fears. It was just that everything seemed so wrong, so unlike she imagined it would be. She didn't even have a place to wash the baby or the clothes she'd brought along for Him. Besides, the streets of Bethlehem were full of Roman soldiers who did not even believe in the one true God.

Joseph helped Mary reach the stable. She lay down on the straw and gasped for breath as she labored to give birth to the Son of God. Late, late that very night, Joseph bent down over Mary's sweaty face and whispered, "Ten fingers! Ten toes! Oh, Mary, He is perfect."

Mary took her newborn in her arms and held Him close. "He is beautiful," she beamed. "Welcome, little Jesus. Welcome to our world. And thank you for coming." Mary wrapped the baby in clean swaddling clothes and laid Him to sleep in the fresh hay beside her. The only cry was the muffled bellow of a calf.

Joseph lay down beside Mary. "I feel like running out and telling everyone what happened here tonight," he said.

Mary pulled him close. "Joseph, God has His own way of sharing this good news. Let's wait and see whom he tells first."

Mary lay awake thinking about all that had happened since the angel Gabriel had appeared to her. She treasured the memories. As she looked at baby Jesus, she thought she heard faint strains of music in the distance. It sounded like no earthly music she'd ever heard. "Joseph," she whispered, "do you hear music? It almost sounds like angels singing." But Joseph didn't answer. He was fast asleep.

As Mary drifted off to sleep, the chorus filled the cold night air: "Glory to God in the highest, and on earth, peace, goodwill to men."

Joseph and Mary stayed in Bethlehem until baby Jesus was sturdy enough to travel. On the way home they passed through the city of Jerusalem. There they stopped at the temple to dedicate Jesus to the Lord.

An old man named Simeon lived in Jerusalem. Simeon had been praying all his life for the savior God had promised. Simeon hoped to see this savior himself. In fact, God had once given him a promise that he would see the savior before he died.

When Mary and Joseph arrived at the temple with baby Jesus, Simeon was there, too. He hobbled back to Mary on his cane and gently lifted the baby from her arms. "You kept your promise, Lord 1" Simeon said. He was so excited he almost shouted. "This boy is the Light that will shine upon all nations of the world and will be the King of Israel."

Mary did not know how to respond. She stood there in astonishment, marvelling at Simeon's words Simeon turned to her and looked directly into her eyes His expression was tender and loving.

"Mary," he said, "Your son will be hated by many people in this country They will make Him suffer in a way that will make you very sad, so sad it will feel like a sword piercing your own heart. But many other people will believe in Jesus. They will know He is God's greatest Gift to the world! His love and joy will fill their lives. His life and death will be like keys to open secret places of the heart and make dreams come true."

As Mary listened to Simeon, she tried to imagine what was going to happen in the coming years. She imagined the time and energy she would pour into raising Jesus, the joy she would feel watching Him grow, the disappointment when people did not understand who He was. Mary imagined the sword that might one day be thrust into Jesus' side. She knew she would feel the pain in her own heart.

"Can I possibly bear all this?" she asked herself "Am I willing to be a part of God's plan after all?"

Simeon returned baby Jesus to the arms of His mother. Mary's mind was racing. "Dear Lord," she prayed silently. "I am just beginning to understand what it means to serve You. I once thought it meant You would fill my life with miracles, that things would always go right. I was so eager to receive Your blessings. Now I'm beginning to see that the greatest blessings of life often come in ways we do not expect. Serving You will mean devoting myself to the ordinary things, like mothers do all day long, and being willing to trust You even when dreams seem to die. Lord God, You specialize in doing the impossible. Make these things possible in my life."

Holding her baby to her breast, Mary thought about the glorious things that lay behind her and the difficult things still ahead of her. The greatest miracle of all was happening in her own heart.

You can find the story of Mary in the New Testament
in the gospels of Matthew, chapters 1–2 and Luke, chapters 1–2.

PETER

The Fisher of Men

By Anne de Graaf

Illustrated by José Pérez Montero

PETER

The Fisher of Men

By Anne de Graaf

Illustrated by José Pérez Montero

There once was a man who knew how to walk on water. There really were two men. One knew and the other tried to know. The one who knew was Jesus. The one who tried to know was called Simon Peter. He was a fisherman.

It happened one night after Simon and some of Jesus' other fnends set off in a boat. Jesus didn't go with them. He wanted to climb a nearby mountain and pray.

"Cross the lake," Jesus told His men. "I'll meet up with you later." Simon and several of the others had often gone night fishing. It was the best time for catching fish. The lake was called the Sea of Galilee. They knew the hills around the lake often trapped winds. At night these winds brought storms.

“I feel the wind changing again,” Simon said to his brother Andrew. The two men watched the sun sizzle into the water to the east. The lake seemed calm, but the two fishermen knew better.

Before long, a storm hit. The wind whipped the waves around the tiny boat! The men strained at the oars. It did no good. The boat went where the storm took it.

“What should we do?’ Simon shouted at John. They were the leaders of the group. But John just shook his head.

In the darkest part of the night, the storm went wild Then suddenly, one of the men yelled. “I see a ghost, Look, there’s something walking on water!”

But of course, there's no such thing as ghosts. The person they saw passing by the boat was Jesus.

"No, how can it be?" the men said to each other They were very afraid. The wind howled in their ears. The sea spray splashed their eyes. They held on to the boat for dear life.

Jesus called out, "Don't be afraid! It's just Me, Jesus," The wind roared. The waves formed walls around the boat. One of the little group of scared men stood up.

It was Simon. "Why, it is Jesus!" he said to the others. He stepped toward the side of the boat and took a closer look.

Jesus' feet barely touched the water. But He did not sink. The waves seemed not to touch Jesus. Wind blew His hair. But Jesus stood tall and strong.

Simon called out, "Lord, if it is You, tell me to come to You on the water."

Jesus said, "Come!"

Simon put one foot over the side. It went down, down, down, then stopped. Then he swung his second leg over and stood up. He did not sink!

Simon felt his back grow warm. He took a step. Then another and another. He watched Jesus the whole time. Simon was walking on water!

But after a few steps, he heard the wind howling. He felt the cold spray on his face. And he looked down. Then Simon forgot to trust Jesus and be brave. Instead of looking at Jesus, he looked at the waves. "How can I, just an ordinary fisherman, walk on water?" he wondered. That's when Simon began to sink. "Help! Lord, save me!" he screamed.

Right away, Jesus reached out and grabbed him. Jesus said, "Oh Simon, Simon! I told you not to be afraid! Why did you stop trying?"

Jesus and Simon climbed back into the boat. The storm stopped The sea grew calm. Simon shook his head. Had it all been a dream? He looked up at Jesus, then out at the still sea.

As Simon watched the water, he thought about the very first time Jesus told him not to be afraid. He had looked over calm waves then, too.

On that first morning, just after sunrise, Simon had been watching the lake. Early morning mist rose off the water. "Something is different today," he said to himself. But he didn't know what.

The sea gulls caw-cawed. The rosy sun spread its light. Simon sighed. He helped his brother Andrew haul the boat up onto the beach. All night long they had fished, working together with the two sons of Zebedee, James and John The men had worked hard, but caught nothing. When Andrew said he was going for a walk, Simon said nothing Thinking hard about his funny feeling, Simon just picked up one of the torn nets. He started mending it.

Hours passed, and Andrew still didn't come back to help his brother. Finally, Simon heard a group of people coming his way. He looked up and saw Andrew break from the crowd and run toward him. "Here He comes, Simony You must stop and listen to Him."

"You mean He's the one who keeps you from helping me mend the nets?" Simon growled. He waved the wooden needle at his brother. A torn net hung over his other arm.

As Andrew turned to join the crowd again, Simon called him back. "Your the big fisherman roared. 'Come help me wash this net."

Andrew did as his brother told him. But he didn't want to Andrew kept looking over at the crowd which was heading their way.

For the rest of the morning Simon and Andrew threw the nets in and out of the water, rinsing them clean. As Simon bent over one net, picking out pieces of seaweed, he saw a shadow on the sand. He looked up. Simon saw a man standing by him.

"That's Him," he heard Andrew whisper.

"Your boat," the man said. At the sound of His voice, Simon shivered. "May I please use your boat?"

Simon nodded. He and Andrew helped the man into the boat, then pushed it into the water. Simon had no choice but to wait, as the man went on teaching the crowd on the beach.

When He had finished, the man turned to Simon. "Push the boat out mto deeper water. Then let down your nets."

"But we've fished hard all night and caught nothing." Then Simon looked into the man's dark eyes again. He changed his mind. "But because You say so, I'll do it."

Simon and Andrew threw the nets overboard. Suddenly, the boat sagged. "Whoa! Look at this!" The two fishermen couldn't believe their eyes. The nets were about to break, they were so full of fish.

"Over here! Over here!" They called their partners, James and John, to bring the other boat.

"I don't believe it!"

The men sweated and strained to heave all the fish into the two boats. Even so, both boats were so full, they began to sink! That's when Simon stumbled over to Jesus.

He fell to his knees and said, "You don't even know me! Don't do this for me, I'm nobody special. Why, I'm no good at all!" Simon waved his hand at the huge catch. Fish slapped the sides of both boats. Some even wiggled their way back into the water. The men stood with their mouths open. They had never seen a catch like this.

That's when Jesus said to Simon for the first time, "Don't be afraid. Come, follow Me and I'll make you fishers of men." These were the most important words in Simon's life. He would hear them again and again and still never forget.

Simon looked back over the sea. The mist had lifted. A tingly feeling ran up his back. Now he knew why the day would be different.

As soon as the boats were beached, Simon left everything behind. He even left the catch in the boats, and that's not an easy thing for a fisherman to do. Then he followed Jesus. After that day when Simon first met Jesus, everything changed. Simon wanted something more than just to catch fish. He and Andrew, together with their partners James and John, became Jesus' best friends. They followed Him from village to village, listening and learning.

It wasn't easy. They had left everything behind. They weren't even sure who Jesus was. All Simon knew was he had to hear more.

The crowds grew larger every time Jesus taught. The people watched Jesus make sick people better, over and over again. Simon could not believe his eyes. He did know, though, that every time Jesus looked at him, Simon wanted to please Him. Still, when all these people asked him who Jesus was, Simon wasn't so sure.

One day Jesus asked the men around Him,"Tell Me, who do the people say I am?"

His followers sat in a circle. "Some say John the Baptist. Others say Elijah. Some say You're one of the great men from the past, come back to life."

Jesus said, "But what about you? Who do you say I am?"

The dark eyes rested on Simon. He felt pushed from inside to say, "You're the Messiah, the Son of the living God." He held his breath.

Jesus said, "Ah, Simon, the only way you could know this is if My Father in heaven told you. You're blessed by God in a special way. Now listen, your name is Simon, but from now on you shall be called Peter." That meant "Rock."

"I'm calling you Peter because someday you'll lead the people who follow Me. They are My Church. You'll become the rock on which the Church is built. That means when you're their leader, it will be your job to teach people what is right and wrong You'll be the most important person in building up the group who will follow Me."

Peter's eyes grew round The others looked at him strangely. "Is this what it means to be a 'fisher of men'?" he asked himself Now Peter knew one thing for sure. The next time someone asked who Jesus was, he wouldn't shake his head He knew Jesus came straight from heaven. He was God's very own Son!

Peter followed Jesus all over the country, watching and learning The weeks became months. For over two years Peter listened to Jesus The more he learned the more he wanted to know.

Strange and wonderful things happened during those years. Peter watched Jesus help blind people to see and the crippled to walk.

One day Peter even saw the two great men Moses and Elijah visit Jesus from heaven. They stood and talked with Jesus on a mountaintop, all white and shining!

Afterward Jesus said, "Don't tell anyone what you've seen today until I've risen from the dead."

Peter and his friends didn't know what Jesus meant. " 'Risen from the dead'? Is Jesus going to die?" they asked. It didn't take long for them to find out.

Not everyone liked Jesus. He had enemies. Most of the religious leaders hated Jesus. They wanted to kill Him. There were also so many people who loved Jesus, though, that Peter and his friends thought Jesus was safe. They were wrong.

It happened one night in Jerusalem. Jesus and His friends had eaten dinner together. All evening long Jesus had talked about how He would soon be killed, but then come back to life again. "Tonight, none of you will help Me," Jesus said.

Peter didn't like that kind of talk. He stood up and said angrily, "What do You mean? The others might leave You, but

I'll always stand by You"

Jesus shook His head. "Ah, Peter. Don't you know? Tonight, before the rooster crows, you'll say you never knew Me. You'll do this three times."

"No! No, I'd die for You. I'll never, ever lie about knowing You!" The other men said the same. Jesus said nothing.

After dinner, Jesus and His men climbed a hill to a special garden. Jesus wanted to pray to God. He was very sad. His heart felt as though it would break and He had a huge lump in His throat. He didn't want to die. He asked Peter, James and John, "Stay with Me and pray."

Jesus prayed as hard as He could. He was so torn up inside about what He had to do, Jesus sweat tears of blood. But where was Peter? Where was the "Rock"? He had fallen asleep!

"Peter! Couldn't you even stay awake to help Me pray? A terrible night is ahead of us. Try and help Me"

Peter tried and tried. More than anything, he wanted to help Jesus The night was warm, though. No matter how hard he tried not to, something made Peter close his eyes as he leaned up against a tree. The next thing he knew, Jesus was shaking him awake for a third time.

"Are you still asleep? Look, it's too late! Here come My enemies to take Me away!"

Peter looked where Jesus pointed. Soldiers, A mob of angry people headed their way. They carried torches and swords! Peter jumped up. Fear turned his stomach over. He grabbed Andrew. "They wouldn't dare take Jesus" Both men knew Jesus had many friends, but He also had many enemies.

"Where can we run?" Peter looked around the moonlit garden. There was nowhere to go. They were trapped!

One of the men who had been a follower of Jesus walked with the soldiers and priests. He had told Jesus' enemies, "The one I go up to is the one you should take prisoner."

This man's name was Judas. Peter watched Judas hug Jesus and kiss Him on the cheek. He said, "Teacher"

"Do what you have to,' Jesus said quietly.

Then the soldiers moved in. They grabbed Jesus and started taking Him away. "This is a nightmare!" Peter gasped. Jesus' enemies acted angry and mean. "You can't take the Teacher away" Peter bellowed.

Peter shook himself, quickly looked around and grabbed his short sword. Then he ran toward the crowd. Waving the sword, Peter yelled, "Leave the Teacher alone!"

With a mighty "Swish" the sword cut off a slave's ear! Peter stared at the ear. Then he remembered Jesus' talk about death. The bad dream was coming true!

"Stop it" Jesus cried. "Put your sword back. Don't you know that anyone who uses the sword, usually will die by the sword?" Then Jesus touched the slave's ear and made him better!

He turned to Peter, "If I wanted to, I could ask My Father to send thousands of angels to fight for Me. But no, I'm going to do My Father's mission If you fight them, I can't do what I came here to do. Peter," He looked into the fisherman's eyes, "don't be afraid."

Just as Jesus finished speaking, the guards dragged Him away. By then all the other disciples had fled. Peter felt torn Should he run and hide as the others had, or should he try and help Jesus somehow? "I can't follow! They might come and take me away toot" So Peter ran and hid behind an olive tree. Despite Jesus' words, the big man trembled with fear.

Peter waited until the soldiers had marched down to the bottom of the hill. Then he followed, hiding behind trees and houses as he went. The priests and soldiers brought Jesus to a courtyard.

There the guards built a fire to keep themselves warm. The priests and other religious leaders began to question Jesus. Peter didn't know what to do. "What will happen to Jesus?" he grumbled to himself. He took a deep breath and crept into the courtyard. Peter sat down by the fire with the guards. It would be a long night.

He hoped no one would notice him. But a servant girl stared at Peter for a few moments. She said, "You were with Jesus of Nazareth."

Peter looked over his shoulders. "I hope no one heard her" he thought. "If the guards find out who I am, they'll kill me."

"No! No!" he said loud enough for everyone to hear. "I don't know what you're talking about!"

Peter hugged himself. He was the only one of Jesus' disciples in the courtyard All the others had run away. "I'd better not stay by this fire," he thought.

Peter walked toward the gateway. There another girl saw him. She said, "This man was with Jesus."

Peter swore, "I don't even know Him!"

After a little while, a group of men standing nearby came up to Peter. One of the men knew the slave whose ear Peter had sliced off. "Didn't I see you in the garden with that Jesus? I'm sure of it," he said. "You're one of Jesus' friends. Why, we can hear you're both from the same place just by the way you talk!"

By now, Peter was so afraid, he swore again and again. "I don't even know the man!"

No sooner were the words out of Peter's mouth, than he heard a rooster crow Just then, Jesus turned and looked straight at Peter. Peter's heart broke. Jesus had said, "Before the rooster crows, you'll say you don't know Me three times."

Peter hid his face in his hands. It seemed as though his very world had crumbled. He staggered out of the courtyard, weeping every step of the way."

During the dark days ahead, Peter felt himself grow old and tired. The day after Jesus was arrested, His enemies killed Him, hanging Jesus on a cross. Peter watched it happen. It burned him inside. It hurt so much, Peter felt numb.

He and some of the other men and women went into hiding. They were afraid the soldiers and priests might take them away and kill them. "If they can arrest and kill Jesus, they could do it to us," Peter told them.

They had forgotten what Jesus so often had taught them, "Don't be afraid."

A few days later, a woman who belonged to this group of Jesus' followers burst through the door of their hiding place. She ran up to Peter and his old fishing partner, John. "Something terrible has happened! They've taken Jesus' body away! He's not in the cave anymore!"

Peter looked at John John looked at Peter. Without another word, the two dashed off to the garden where Jesus was buried in a cave. They tore down the streets. Peter had never run so fast before in his life. He panted and raced, but John still beat him. At the cave, they stopped.

John looked in. Peter shot past him and entered the cave. "Nothing" He panted at John. "She's right. There's nothing here but the cloths Jesus was wrapped in!"

The two men bent double, trying to catch their breath. "It's no use," John said. "We'd better get back to the others."

After a few moments they left, shaking their heads. "The priests must have stolen His body" Peter clenched his fists. "I have to find out what's going on!" Peter wouldn't have long to wait.

That evening the men and women huddled together in the attic room where they were hiding. "Do you think the soldiers will kill us, too?" they asked each other. No one knew. They had locked the doors to be on the safe side.

Suddenly, a shape passed through the wall! It was Jesus! The men gasped. The women screamed!

"Peace!" Jesus told them And again He said, "Don't be afraid, it's Me." He showed them the sores on His hands and side.

"It really is Jesus" The horror on Peter's face turned to joy. He and the rest were so happy they didn't know what to say. Peter felt a great weight lift off his shoulders. "Oh Teacher, Teacher," he cried. The huge fisherman fell to the floor on his knees. Tears streamed down his cheeks.

Peter saw Jesus several times after He rose from the dead. One of those times was when Peter and some of his friends wanted to get some food for the others. So they went fishing. They spent all night on the lake. By morning their boat was still empty.

"Caught anything?" A stranger called out from the beach.

"No," the fishermen answered. The stranger stood with the rising sun behind him. Peter and the others could not see that actually, he was Jesus!

The men brought the boat closer to shore. Jesus said, "Throw your net over the righthand side of the boat! Then you'll find some fish."

The men were so tired they didn't even argue. Within minutes the net came back full! John squinted at the stranger. "It's Him!" he shouted. "It's the Lord!" John grabbed Peter.

"You're right!" Peter said. "Only Jesus could have filled the net like this. It's the same miracle as what happened on that first day I met Him!" Peter quickly pulled on some clothes and jumped into the water. He forgot to breathe, he swam so hard. "It's really Him, it's really Him!"

He kept saying to himself.

Once on shore, Peter wouldn't leave Jesus' side. The others brought in the boat. Peter helped Jesus fry some fish for them over a fire While they ate, John said to Peter, "This is just like old times, isn't it?" Peter nodded and grinned, his mouth full of fish.

After the meal, Jesus called Peter to one side. He wanted to talk in private "Peter, do you really love Me? Do you love Me more than these others do?"

Peter gasped. "Of course, Lord! Why, You know I love You."

"Then take care of My sheep." Jesus was telling Peter to take care of all the people he would someday lead closer to God. Jesus asked His question three times. Each time, Peter answered yes.

Jesus finished by saying that Peter would indeed lead Jesus' followers well. He also said that Peter would die a terrible death. When Peter's eyes grew round, Jesus said, "Don't be afraid. Just follow Me."

Even though Peter had seen and heard Jesus with his own eyes and ears, he still felt afraid. He and the others were scared the priests and soldiers might take them away and kill them.

They just did not know what to do. Every time Jesus saw them, He said, "Don't be afraid." It didn't help much until Jesus added a promise. "Soon I'll send you a Helper."

On the day when the Helper arrived, Peter finally stopped being afraid.

He was upstairs praying with his friends. Suddenly a sound like the blowing of a strong wind filled the house. "Whoosh!"

"What's that?" the others asked. Small lights like flames rested on the heads of Peter, John, Andrew and the others. It was the Helper, God's Holy Spirit, come to make Jesus' followers strong and brave!

Peter shook himself. What had happened? He didn't care anymore about being arrested! "We must tell more people about Jesus!" he told his friends. "No matter what, they must know!"

The people outside had heard the strange sound like wind. Because this was a busy city, they came from countries all over the world. In their different languages they asked, "We heard an odd sound hit your house. What happened?"

Peter spoke and no one could believe what they heard! "How can that simple fisherman speak so many different languages?" In the ears of thousands of people it sounded as if Peter came from their very own hometowns.

"Listen," he shouted. "Jesus, the great Teacher Jesus is really the Son of God! You had Him killed, but now God has brought Him back to life again! Don't be afraid! Believe in Him and He'll change your lives! Follow Jesus!"

Peter's message cut into the hearts of over three thousand people. They all felt sorry about living bad lives. They wanted to start over again. They asked Jesus to forgive them and help them. These were the first Christians and Peter became their first leader.

All the people who believed in Jesus prayed together. They learned from Peter and his friends. Those who were rich shared their money and things with those who were poor. No man or woman was better off than any other.

Even though there were many who believed what Peter preached, many more called him a liar. The same religious leaders who killed Jesus, wanted to kill Peter.

Thanks to the Holy Spirit, Peter wasn't afraid anymore. "The most important thing is to share Jesus with as many people as possible!" He traveled far and wide to share the Good News.

All the same, it didn't take long before Peter's enemies had him arrested. The first time this happened, Peter showed such bravery, everyone was amazed.

"He's just a fisherman, how does he know what he's talking about!"

"Such courage,"

"Ah yes, wasn't he with that Jesus?" And his enemies let Peter go free.

The second time Peter was arrested he had a harder time of it. The terrible King Herod did not like the Christians. He had already killed James, one of Peter's fishing friends. Now he wanted to kill Peter. "Arrest him! Chain that man to a soldier so he won't get away!"

`We warned him to stop talking about that Jesus!"

"Now he'll learn his lesson,"

Poor Peter! He sat in a damp and dirty prison cell. The next day Herod would surely have him killed in order to please Peter's enemies. Chained to two soldiers as he slept, Peter didn't have much reason to hope.

Even so, Peter wasn't afraid. Peter trusted Jesus. The other Christians also trusted Jesus. They prayed and waited, hoping that somehow their leader might go free.

That night as Peter slept, a very strange thing happened' Someone shook him. He opened his eyes and saw a bright angel! "Hurry!" the angel said. "Get up and come with me!"

As the angel spoke, the chains fell off Peter's arms' "Put your cloak on and follow me," the angel said.

Peter did as the angel told him "I must be dreaming," he thought as he walked right past the snoring guards. "No one can see me!"

Once outside, the iron gate leading to the city opened all by itself! Then the angel disappeared. Peter stood still, waiting for the sounds of shouting and running feet. "Nothing! How can that be?" he asked himself.

"God set me free and the guards didn't see a thing!" Peter ran to a friend's house. Many people were gathered there, praying for Peter.

He knocked on the door. A servant came, but she was so excited to hear Peter's voice, she ran off before opening the door!

Peter's friends told the servant, "You're crazy' There's no way Peter can be standing outside. We're praying for him right now!"

But Peter kept knocking Finally his friends opened up for him."Peter I" Everyone hugged him and wanted to hear his story.

The next morning the king searched for Peter, but could not find him. The guards scratched their heads. Then the evil King Herod punished his guards by putting them all to death.

In the years to come, the Chnstians' enemies became more and more terrible. They arrested and killed many believers. Peter led the Christians bravely. He was no longer the unsure, stubborn fisherman Jesus had first met.

Peter became a true fisher of men. Peter's words helped people all over the world to want to know more about Jesus. Peter even let others hurt him, rather than say he did not love Jesus. He led the Christians, and whenever their enemies made them suffer, Peter felt the pain, too.

When Peter died, he went to heaven. Many people think Peter died on a cross, just like Jesus. They say Peter's enemies hung him upside down. At that final moment, no doubt Jesus was right at Peter's side. Maybe Jesus even whispered the same words He had already spoken so often to His friend the fisherman. "Don't be afraid, Peter. Follow Me."

You can find the story of Peter in the New Testament in the gospels of Matthew, Mark, Luke and John, as well as in Acts, chapters 1–15.

MARY MAGDALENE

A Woman Who Showed Her Gratitude

By Marlee Alex

Illustrated by José Pérez Montero

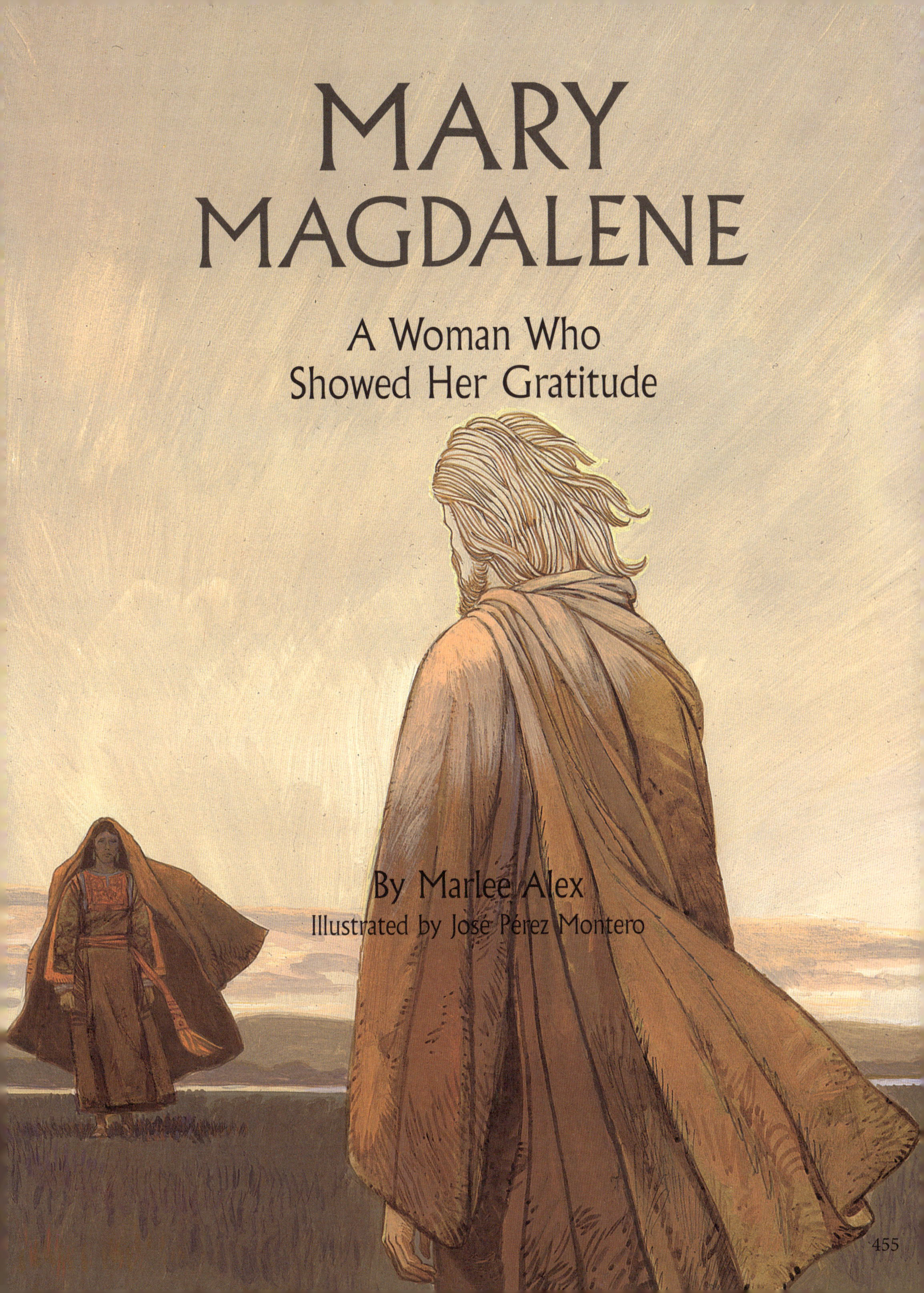

MARY MAGDALENE

A Woman Who Showed Her Gratitude

By Marlee Alex

Illustrated by José Pérez Montero

The towers of Jerusalem, usually splashed in sunlight at that time of day, were wrapped in gray. A chill pervaded the city. Mary Magdalene shivered as she trudged up a hillside just outside the city wall. She pulled her cloak tightly around her shoulders, but felt no warmer, for her heart was as cold as the wind. To Mary it seemed an eternity before she reached the hilltop of Golgotha, »The Place of the Skull.« It was not a hill people climbed over in order to get to the other side. Golgotha was climbed for one of two reasons to die or to watch someone else die.

»After this, nothing in the world can ever make things right amain,« murmured Mary to herself Her words flew away through the turbulent air. No one heard what she said.

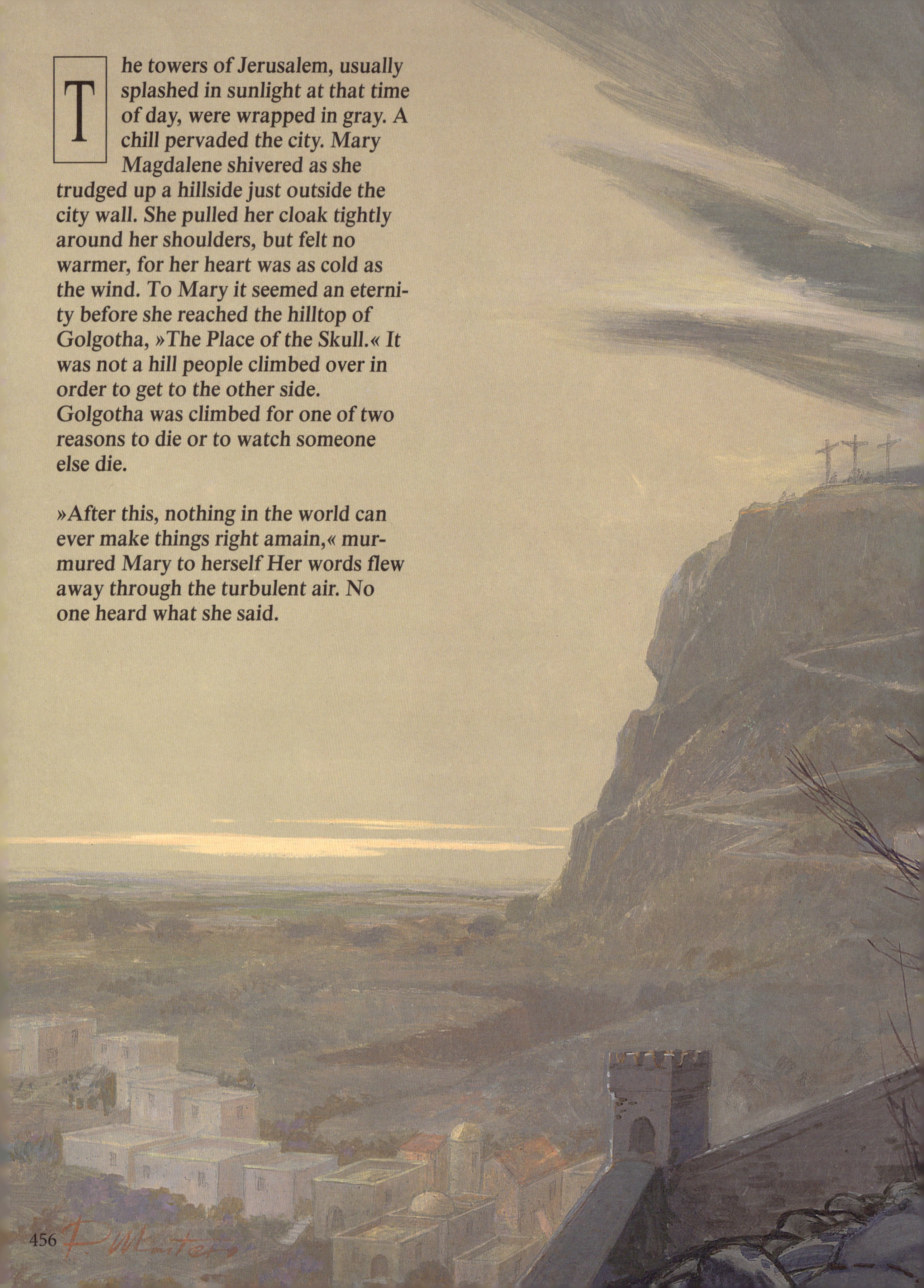

JESUS
REX

Several other women stood huddled together on the hilltop. When she reached them, Mary Magdalene felt brokenhearted and began to sob. A second woman, also named Mary, stood close by. But the gentle eyes of this woman revealed acceptance of what she witnessed, in spite of the terrible suffering. Two other women were clinging to each other for comfort. But Mary Magdalene could find no comfort.

The Roman soldiers milling about had no sympathy for the women. »These women should be forced to leave,« one of them muttered.

Another soldier laughed in return, »No one should be allowed to mourn for this phony Jewish king.«

a The sky grew darker and raindrops spattered upon the sparse grass. Mary Magdalene looked up at the rough wooden cross standing between two other crosses on the top of Golgotha. The cross was the Roman method of putting criminals to death. Mary watched as the Person she loved more than anyone else in the world, a Man called Jesus, hung dying upon that center cross. He was in tremendous pain. His chest heaved as Mary watched. It seemed to her He was trying to catch His breath in order to speak.

Mary Magdalene moved closer to the foot of Jesus' cross. From the day she first met Jesus she had stayed as close as possible to Him. She had followed Him everywhere, helping His disciples in practical ways, listened carefully to His teaching, and witnessed miracle after miracle as He ministered to sick and sad people. Now, even as Jesus died, Mary wanted to be close to Him and hear any last words He might say. But instead, Mary's ears were filled with the sounds of hoarse laughter and crude jokes hurled at Jesus by the Roman soldiers, Jewish leaders, and even one of the thieves hanging on the cross beside Him.

Suddenly Jesus cried out, but not toward those waiting impatiently for Him to die He cried toward heaven itself, »Father, forgive these people, for they do not understand what they are doing.«

Mary Magdalene gasped. She thought to herself, »I cannot have heard Him right! Or did I? Did I really hear Him ask God to forgive these hypocrites, these murderers? No, Jesus! You brought only healing and mercy to the world! They are guilty.« Mary wanted to cry out loud, »No! Never! Never forgive them for this!«

Before Mary could choke out the bitter words, however, her mind was flooded with memories. It was not so very long ago, since she herself had received God's forgiveness. At that time it had seemed to her as incredible as His words did now. Yet, it had tasted sweet as honey when Jesus looked directly into her eyes and promised, »Your sins are forgive!«

She had thought, »No man has ever dared look into my eyes at all. And certainly no one else has ever looked at me with acceptance, forgiveness or a love like this.«

The only glances Mary Magdalene had ever drawn from men were lustful; from other women she had received only scorn Children had usually looked at her in fear or curiosity, while their mothers had hurried them off in opposite directions or across the street. Mary never had a hope of raising a family of her own or havmg the kind of life most people take for granted.

P. Montero

For as long as she could remember she had been tormented by a demon and ruled by its wicked fancies. No one in her hometown of Magdala knew how it had started. But Mary had grown up, a homeless girl, known for her fits of rage and for the way she earned a living by selling her body to please men.

People had occasionally hissed at Mary in the street, »For God's sake, girl, take hold of yourself and start behaving decently!« Little had they realized how greatly she had wished she could do right instead of wrong. There were times when she had tried to master the demon within her and turn from her sinful way of life, the only kind of life she had ever known.

At one such time Mary had tried her hardest to drive the demon out of her soul and to clean up her life. For a while, her efforts had worked. But just when she had seemed closest to becoming a respectable person, the demon returned. Finding her life clean, yet empty, it had moved right back into its old home again. But this time it had brought six other demons with it. And these six were far worse than the first one.

Then Mary's life had become more miserable than ever. There were days she had struggled against the demons, but whenever the struggle grew too fierce, she had lost complete control of her body and mind. Thrown into a wild frenzy at those times, Mary Magdalene would writhe on the ground until all her strength had been drained. It had happened again and again until the last remnant of peace within her had finally been destroyed.

There had been one old woman in Magdala who had pitied Mary, but she had no idea how to help her Nevertheless, Mary felt she knew at least one truth: no one would ever truly love her.

Then something totally unexpected had happened. Jesus of Nazareth had crossed her path in Magdala. As he passed within an arm's reach of her, the seven demons had begun to scream and wrestle with each other, shaking Mary's body as never before The townspeople following Jesus had learned to keep out of Mary's way and ignore her. And not even Jesus had seemed to notice her that clay. He had disappeared in the crowd.

Finally Mary had collapsed on the dusty street By the time she had recovered, no one else was around. The crowds had dissipated into other streets and alleys. Jesus had already left town. But right away Mary had known something was different; her body and mind were at peace, no longer haunted by the evil spirits. They had been driven away by the very presence of Jesus.

Mary had picked herself up off the street in Magdala that day wondering, »What happened? Can I be sure the demons are gone for good? They will most likely return unless the emptiness in my soul is filled with something better.« Mary had known that trying to live a decent life on her own or »be good« would not change things. So she had asked everyone she met, »Who was that Man? Where was He from? How can I find Him?«

They had answered, »He is called Jesus. He is a prophet from Nazareth who claims to be the Son of God.« Mary knew holy men could have her stoned to death for the sinful way she lived. But that day she made a decision, »I would rather face death than the terror of the returning demons. I'm going to find that Man and talk to Him.«

Many weeks passed before Mary had heard the news, >Jesus has returned.«

»There is a rumor He will dine tonight at the home of a Jewish leader,« an old woman had told her. »Ha! That's a switch! He usually eats with tax collectors and sinners! The woman had laughed spitefully. She had not even recognized Mary as the young woman who so recently had been known as the worst sinner in town.

Mary had continued questioning people until she found the house where Jesus would be dining. A crowd had begun to gather around the door and windows Mary had pressed through the crowd and into the doorway. »I would rather die at the feet of this Man than be tormented for the rest of my life,« she had whispered.

Without thinking she had pushed her way right into the room where Jesus was reclining on a couch by the dinner table. Once in His presence, a surge of hope and gratitude had welled up within her.

Mary sunk to her knees at the end of the couch as tears had spilled from her eyes onto Jesus' bare feet. The tears had glistened like diamonds. Surprisingly, Jesus had not made any attempt to move away from her. Mary had dried away the tears from Jesus' feet with her long dark hair, then began to gently kiss his feet and ankles. Clasping the small, white marble bottle that had always hung on a belt around her waist, Mary had poured its last drops of perfume onto His feet and rubbed them into His skin.

While Jesus had not even been embarrassed by what Mary had done, His Jewish host had felt differently He had grown paler by the minute, for gradually it had dawned on him that this was the woman well known in Magdala for the wicked life she led. He was horrified. »If Jesus were really sent from God,« he had thought to himself, »He would know this woman is a sinner. He would never have allowed her to touch Him like this.«

Jesus had interrupted the man's thoughts. »A certain man owed a friend 500 coins,« He said. »Another man owed the same friend 50 coins. Neither of the men were able to pay back the money they owed. So their friend told them, 'All right, neither of you have to pay me back. You are forgiven your debts:«

Jesus had turned to the Jewish leader. »Now, which of these two men do you suppose will love his friend the most?« He asked.

The Jewish leader had answered. »Well, the one who owed the most money because he would have the most for which to be thankful.«

Jesus had looked directly into the eyes of His host. »You are correct,« He whispered. »And did you see what this woman has just done? When I came into your house you did not offer Me the favor of a basin of water and a towel with which to clean My dusty feet. But she has washed them with her tears and dried them with her hair. You did not greet Me with a kiss on My cheek, but she has kissed My feet and used up her last drops of ointment upon them.

»This woman is driven to express her love because she has much for which to be thankful. But as for the person who thinks he can get along fine by himself or doesn't need God's forgiveness, his love for Me will be weak and feeble. And he will be unwilling to show even the least bit of gratitude.«

The face of the Jewish leader had flushed pink. but Jesus had turned around to Mary and said, »Woman, your sins are forgiven. The faith you have displayed in Me today has saved you. Go in peace.«

As Maly left the house of the Jewish leader that day she had heard the crowd behind her murmuring and questioning each other, »Who is this Man, Jesus, who thinks He has the right to forgive sins?«

Mary Magdalene stood at the foot of the cross on Golgotha where these memories swept through her mind. The wind picked up strength. The day became darker still Mary's thoughts were jarred to the present. Jesus suddenly cried out above her, »Father, into Your hands I commit My Spirit.« Then His body lurched forward, the nails tore the flesh in His hands, and He fell limp upon the cross.

Mary was startled. It didn't seem possible Jesus could be dead. For the first time she drew closer to the other women on the hilltop. As Jesus' body was at last removed from the cross they followed Joseph, the man who carried it, to a new tomb not far away. The women watched as Joseph wrapped Jesus' body in linen and lay it in the clean stone tomb.

»So this is how it is to end,« whispered one of the women.

Mary interrupted, »Oily days ago we followed Jesus from Galilee and listened to the happy shouts of children here in Jerusalem. «Hosanna! Hosanna to the king, the son of David!' they were shouting.«

»Now the parents of these same children have executed our King, Jesus, like a common thief,«continued a third woman.

Mary peered into the dark tomb and saw the still, lifeless body of Jesus lying on the stone slab. Her heart could not accept that there was nothing more to do. »What of the spices or perfumed oil we should wrap into His burial clothes?« she asked It was nearly sunset on that long Friday afternoon, the beginning of the Jewish Sabbath, a day when Jewish people would stop everything in order to worship God.

»There is no time for embalming His body with spices know,« corrected one of the other women. »We will have to wait until sunrise Sunday morning.« So the women returned home to wait.

That night and the next day, the Sabbath, were long ones for the grieving women. Mary Magdalene found it especially difficult to wait. By nature she needed to give expression to the love she felt. And her love for Jesus had been fervent. No one had ever cared for her as Jesus had. She would never stop being devoted to Him, even in death. She desperately wanted to pour out her last expressions of gratitude.

Early Sunday morning before the other women awoke, Mary got up in the darkness and gathered the carefully prepared spices and oils she had made ready before sundown on Friday. In the glow of the approaching dawn she made her way to the tomb on the hillside where Jesus' body lay. Along the way she wondered, »Who will roll away the stone? How will I be able to enter?«

But arriving at the tomb, Mary was amazed to find the large rock had already been rolled away. An angel was sitting on top of it, although Mary did not recognize him as a messenger from God. The angel said to Mary, »Why are you looking in a grave for a man who is alive?« Startled and confused, Mary bent down, and took a long look into the place where she had watched Joseph lay the body of Jesus. The tomb was empty »Someone has taken His body away,« she exclaimed.

»See, Jesus is not here!o!« the angel announced. »He is alive!«

Mary could neither understand, nor believe what she was hearing. She turned and went back the way she had come, trying to make sense of the events of the past three days. Then she noticed a Man approaching her on the path. The sun was rising over the lowest trees behind Him. The radiant sunbeams shone into her eyes as she called out, »You must be the gardener here. Sir, if you have taken the body of Jesus, please tell me where it is. I have come to anoint it with oil and place these spices in His grave clothes.«

The man on the narrow path stepped directly in front of the shining sun. His face was full of light, His expression pure like the sun itself. »Mary'« He said. That voice chimed like music in Mary's ears. It was a voice she recognized, for no one had ever said her name in quite that way except for .. Jesus!

»Lords« Mary exclaimed. She ran to Him and fell at His feet.

»Waist, Mary,« Jesus interrupted. »Don't touch Me yet. I haven't yet ascended to My Father in heaven. But go and tell My other friends you have met Me. Tell those who followed Me to wait in Jerusalem. I'll meet them there Coon.« Then Jesus disappeared from Mary's sight. Her feet nearly flew as she hurried back to the disciples to tell what she had seen.

As a follower of Jesus Christ, Mary Magdalene witnessed that the only people Jesus had no power to forgive were those who believed they were already good enough or those who were too proud to recognize Him as God's Son When Mary expressed her faith in Jesus and received God's forgiveness she was filled with a fervent love for Him.

Mary continuously fed her love for Jesus with acts of gratitude and devotion. She became the first person to meet Jesus after He rose from the dead. She brought the message of joy to Jesus' friends and set an example for all who wish to bring joy to the heart of Jesus Himself.

You can find the story of Mary Magdalene in the New Testament
in the gospels of Mark, chapters 14 and 16; Luke, chapter 7; and John, chapter 12.

PAUL

A Change of Heart

By Anne de Graaf

Illustrated by José Pérez Montero

PAUL

A Change of Heart

By Anne de Graaf

Illustrated by José Pérez Montero

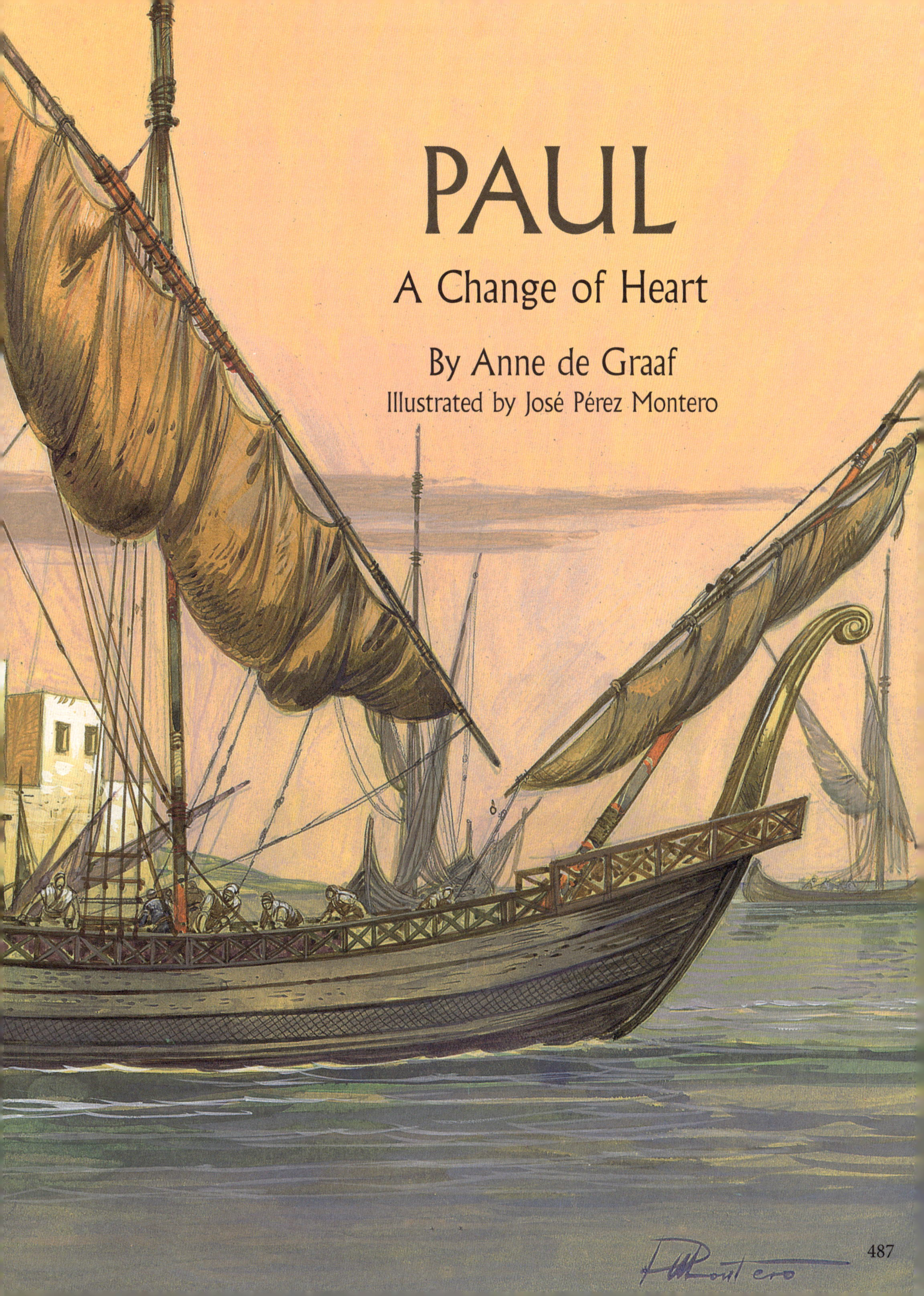

Saul's anger rose in him like a fire. "Stephen has gone too far!" he shook with rage.

Stephen stood in the middle of a great hall. All around him, religious leaders shook their fists. Stephen lifted his hands up high. He reached for something none of them could see.

"Look!" Stephen pointed. "The heavens are opening up. There is Jesus, standing next to God!"

"Enough!" Saul shouted.

"Stone him!"

"We don't want to hear anymore!" the religious leaders cried out.

"Don't listen!" Saul told the rest. They covered their ears and rushed at Stephen. Guards grabbed the prisoner and dragged him out of the city. A mob of angry, yelling people followed. The religious leaders, mcluding Saul, told the people what had happened.

"He says Jesus was the Son of God. He talks as if He were His best friend!"

"He made fun of God!"

As they threw Stephen down the hill, they began stoning him. Saul shouted with the rest, "Kill him before he says anything more against God."

Stephen steadied himself with one hand while the other reached toward heaven. "Lord Jesus!" Stephen said. "Take me, please!"

"Don't listen! He'll poison your minds!" Saul roared.

Stephen's last words were, "Lord, don't hold this against them!" Then Stephen said no more. He had gone to heaven. There he would never again feel the sharp pain of stones.

The crowd threw more rocks until the crumpled body lay half buried. Then, slowly, they backed away, breathing hard. Some shook their heads, "He deserved worse."

A mother pulled her child away. "I want to see, I want to seer the boy cried.

"There's nothing to see," his mother mumbled.

Saul walked with the other religious leaders back to the Temple. As he came alongside the chief priest, he said to the important man, "That was just the beginning. From now on we wage war against the followers of Jesus. Who do they think they are? Again and again they break the Law."

Soon Saul had driven most of the Christians out of Jerusalem. Then he went to the high priest. "If you would give the word, I could make sure these followers of Jesus are stamped out. With a letter from you, I could travel to Damascus and hunt them down." He paused, letting his words sink in.

"I'll bring them back bound to Jerusalem, then throw them into prison. We can punish them as we did Stephen. No one, not one more person than I can help will have to hear anymore about Jesus. His name will be wiped out, His memory forgotten."

So important was Saul's mission that the high priest not only gave him the letter he had asked for, but a special guard as well. Saul rode off toward Damascus. He believed in his heart he was doing the right thing.

What is right and what is wrong? Sometimes our hearts are the only voices which tell us. And sometimes it takes a change of heart before we can learn the truth. This is what happened to Saul. Only then could he grasp what was truly right and what was wrong.

Saul and his guard galloped through the desert. By noon they were within sight of the great city, Damascus. And then, suddenly, a light flashed around Saul.

"Agh!" he screamed and threw his hands up to protect his eyes. His horse reared and Saul tumbled to the ground. He saw nothing. The dazzling light had blinded him!

"Saul! Saul!" he heard a Voice. "Why do you keep hurting Me so much?"

The guards riding with Saul also saw the light. Mouths open, they heard the sound, but could not understand it. Saul knew what the Voice was saying, though. "Who are You?" he cried.

"I am Jesus. I am the One you have been hunting down and hurting."

Saul felt a knife cut into his heart. He had been wrong, All this time, he had wanted so badly to follow the rules. But he had ended up hurting the very Lord he served! The knife of shame twisted as Saul felt his heart change.

"What," he gasped. "What can I do? Lord, tell me what I should do!"

"Get up and go on into Damascus," the Voice said. "There you will be told about My plan for your life." Saul nodded. Then the light was gone.

Silence. Saul heard only the desert wind and the stamp of his horse. He called out to the guards, "Damascus. Take me to Damascus. That's where I must go. Lead me there, will you please?"

Step by step the guards led the blinded Saul into Damascus. There he did not eat or drink anything for three days. Then the Lord sent one of His followers to make Saul better.

And so Saul joined the very followers of Jesus he had sworn to kill. God had changed Saul's heart. Now Saul knew, without a doubt, Jesus was the right Way, the only Way to God.

It was not easy for the Christians to accept Saul as one of their own. Not so long ago he had hunted them down. Now he wanted to come to their prayer meetings.

The followers of Jesus listened to Saul preach, "Jesus is the Christ? He really is the Son of God and He's alive today!"

The religious leaders in Damascus did not like this at all! One of their very own had turned against them. No matter how they argued, though, Saul was able to outwit them. Again and again he proved Jesus is the Son of God. Jesus' Holy Spirit gave Saul the right words.

The Christians in Damascus had no choice. "Just listen to him God has turned an enemy into a friend."

But the religious leaders said, "He's changed from a friend mto an enemy! We must kill Saul before he causes more trouble!"

Word of the plot reached the Chnstians. "Hurry, Saul, we must get you out of Damascus. These religious leaders are serious."

"I know,"Saul sighed. "I used to be one of them."

That night Saul's new friends led him up dark stairs, all the way to the top of the city walls. "They're watching the gates. No one will expect you to escape this way."

Three men held a huge basket as Saul climbed in. "We'll pray for you!"

Saul and a friend of his named Barnabas traveled from one village to another. "Have you heard?" they asked people wherever they went. "God sent His only Son His name is Jesus. If you ask Him to, He will forgive all the bad things you've done You can start over. Believe in Jesus! Ask Him to come live in your hearts. Ask Him today"

It was during this time that Saul changed his name to Paul That was the Roman way of saying his name. So now, whenever the two men entered a village people said, "Paul! Barnabas! Please come teach us what you know We've heard a little, but want to know more."

One of the towns Paul and Barnabas visited was called Lystra. There, Paul and Barnabas taught the people "Believe in Jesus. He can help you with your problems!"

One day a very sick man came to Paul. This man had never been able to walk, As he listened to Paul talk about Jesus, he thought, "Yes, I believe in Jesus. Yes!"

Paul looked at the man and saw he was trusting Jesus. He prayed that God might help the man Then Paul said loudly, "Stand up on your feet."

The man jumped up. He began to walk! The crowd cried, "Paul is a god!"

"So is Barnabas!"

"Nor No!" Paul and Barnabas shouted. This was the last thing they wanted. They had come to pomt people toward Jesus, not themselves.

The crowd finally calmed down. But a few days later, something terrible happened This same crowd who had thought Paul and Barnabas were so wonderful, suddenly turned against them.

The religious leaders wanted very much to cause trouble for Paul and Barnabas. They had secretly told the people, "Paul doesn't know what he's talking about. Don't listen to him. He thinks Jesus is the Son of God He says God loves everyone. That's crazy"

The people did not think for themselves. They did not let their own hearts choose what was right and what was wrong. Instead they let the religious leaders choose for them.

"Kill Paul!"

"Throw rocks at him until he dies!"

"Stone the troublemaker!"

So many angry people. They had hardened their hearts against Paul's message from Jesus They yelled and screamed. yet Paul stood, a hero for Jesus.

When the sharp rocks dug into his back, his legs, his face, he sank to his knees. Paul knew what Stephen had felt The pain dug deep, until finally, Paul could feel no more.

Paul's body lay still The mob had dragged him out of the city. They thought he was dead.

A boy stood over the bruised and bleeding body He stared, tears streaming down his face. "Is Paul dead?" he whispered.

Barnabas and a few others had come to bury Paul's body. Barnabas was just about to answer the boy, when he saw Paul move. "No, Timothy, he's not!" Barnabas shouted. "Look everyone, it's a miracle!" He helped Paul to his feet.

The others could not believe their eyes. Surely Paul had died. Yet there he was, standing up.... and walking "Paul, Oh Paul!" they cried. Young Timothy hugged him with the rest.

As Paul walked back into the city, he put his arm around Timothy He had often seen Timothy listening when he talked about Jesus. The boy never said much, but Paul could tell by his eyes that every word had touched Timothy's heart. Paul looked clown at the boy.

"Lord," he asked. "I wonder if someday I could have a son like this one."

At that same moment, Timothy prayed, "Please, Jesus, let me grow up to be like Paul. I want to learn from him."

Jesus answered both their prayers. About a year later Paul came back to Lystra This time he traveled with a friend called Silas.

Paul asked Timothy to come with him and Silas as they went to different villages Timothy was only too happy to say yes. His heart danced as day after day, month after month, the two became like father and son.

Day after day after day, Paul and his friends sailed from one port to the next. Then they walked down the dusty Roman roads and visited as many villages as they could. Wherever they went, Paul, Silas and Timothy talked about Jesus In many places the people listened God opened their hearts so that they believed in Jesus.

Paul helped set up churches by choosing leaders for the groups of Christians. He taught them to share money with the poor. He helped them feel strong when other people wanted to hurt them for believing in Jesus.

For almost eight years Paul traveled by boat and on foot, from country to country. Often he went back to places where the people needed him most He even managed to be in two places at once He did this by wnting letters to the groups of Christians he could not visit. In this way Paul showed that he still cared and was praying for them.

As Paul traveled, he sometimes stayed with friends. Sometimes he had nowhere to stay and made tents so he could buy food He sometimes left Silas or Timothy behind to help solve problems certain groups were having.

Paul and Silas were always on the move. Over and over again they were forced to leave places by the religious leaders. It did not matter that he had once been one of them. Everywhere Paul went, they found reasons to arrest Paul.

In a town called Philippi the religious leaders told a huge mob to attack Paul and Silas. They beat them with sticks and threw them into prison. Paul and Silas lay on the cold stone floor, their hands chained. The guards had locked their feet between huge blocks of wood. They could not move at all! What do you think they did?

They sang songs! Paul and Silas were happy. They knew that Jesus takes very special care of people who are hurt because they believe in Him He stands right by them and comforts them so much, they feel joyful enough to sing And that is just what Paul did.

“We love Jesus, praise His name. Jesus, Jesus, thank You for standing by us’” On into the night the two men sang. They sang their hearts out while all the other prisoners listened.

Around midnight something very strange happened. A terrible roar rocked the prison! The earthquake shook the prison so hard, all the cell doors came flying open! Then the chains binding the prisoners unlocked. God had set the prisoners free!

When the jailer saw this, he trembled with fear. “Who are you?” he asked. He fell down at Paul’s feet. “Please,” he begged. “Tell me what has happened here tonight. I overheard you talking to the other prisoners about being saved. What does that mean? What do I have to do to be saved?”

Paul looked at Silas. They knew that this man’s change of heart was an even greater miracle than the earthquake. Paul smiled at the frightened jailer. “Believe in the Lord Jesus and you will be saved. So will your family.”

The jailer did believe. He took Silas and Paul that very night to his home. There he washed their sores and wounds, then gave them food to eat. Then the Jailer and his family prayed to Jesus and asked Him into their hearts.

Paul wished that everyone they spoke to would believe as the jailer and his family had. When a group of Paul's enemies started chasing him from one village to the next, Paul hardly had time to teach anymore.

"There must be a way we can talk to more people about Jesus," Paul said to Silas.

"You could leave alone and cross the sea to Athens," Silas said. "That way Timothy and I could finish what you've started here. And you would be safe."

"Yes," Paul said. "That's a good idea. I can't be wasting so much time running and hiding. I don't like us splitting up, but maybe it's the only way. We must talk to more people about Jesus."

So once again, Paul sailed away This time he traveled to Athens, a very old Greek city. There, the people prayed to many different gods. The Greeks had gods of the sun and moon and sea and war and peace and love and hate and rocks and fire and anything else you could think of.

"There is only one God!" Paul told them Some of the Greeks listened and wanted to know more.

"You Greeks have made up gods to everything," Paul said. "Why, you even have a temple for the Unknown God. Well that's my God And He's the only one you need to have. This God sent His Son Jesus. Let me tell you about Him...."

So Paul taught the Greeks. But many of them did not believe Paul. "Only one God? Ha ha! Paul is crazy! Don't listen to him!"

"I have better things to do then talk to people who won't hear me," Paul said. Together with the Greeks who did believe him, Paul set off to visit other islands in the area.

By sea and on foot, Paul traveled Everywhere he went, Paul told people about Jesus. It was the most important news he could give them.

Greece was not the only place where Paul ran into people who believed in other gods. In Ephesus, part of the country we now call Turkey, Paul met people who believed in a god named Diana They had built many statues and temples to Diana.

When Paul arrived in Ephesus, he liked it right away. There, many people wanted to hear his Good News about Jesus. They made Paul feel welcome. "Please teach us more about what all this means," they asked.

Paul stayed in Ephesus for two years. During that time, many, many people heard Paul speak. God helped them believe by giving Paul the power to make sick people better. Sometimes all Paul had to do was touch them and pray, and they would be healed!

There was one group of people, though, who did not like Paul. These were the people who wanted to worship Diana, rather than the one God. Some of these men had become rich by selling silver statues of Diana to the people.

"Thanks to Paul, we're not making as much money anymore," they complained.

"Yes, Paul has ruined our business by getting the people to believe in Jesus. Now no one wants to buy our statues!"

"Let's get rid of Paul" The more these men shouted and grumbled, the angrier they became. "Let's go find Paul! We'll teach him a lesson!"

The mob went to the place where Paul taught the people. They yelled at him and started throwing rocks. "There he is Stop the troublemaker!" they screamed.

Finally an official stopped the riot. No one was badly hurt.

Soon after this Paul left Ephesus. But the group of believers he left behind was one of the strongest in the area. They had learned the hard lesson that there is no middle road. Either you believe in Jesus or you don't.

Later Paul would write the Ephesians, helping his good friends there to grow even closer to God.

These letters by Paul were very important. Even with the help of friends like Timothy and Silas Paul could not be everywhere at once. Paul's letters helped the people who had heard him and believed, to follow the Way.

"The Way" is living a life the way Jesus wants us to. Following the Way means loving enemies, praying to Jesus, and starting over whenever we make mistakes. Most of all, it means loving God more than anyone or anything else.

Paul made this clear in his letters. Often he and Timothy would ride from village to village. Whenever they spoke to people about Jesus, it was as if they were planting seeds of truth in their hearts.

When Paul had to leave new friends, he sent them letters. These letters acted as water for the seeds. The words were read and reread by many of the believers. God used these letters to help the seeds of truth grow into rich flowers of faith.

Men and women, children, the rich and the poor, everyone who wanted to believe, did. Inside them all there grew

this feeling that yes, of course, Jesus really is the Son of God!

This is the Way. The more people Paul and Timothy and the other followers of Jesus spoke with, the more believed. And just as the wind spreads the seeds of a flower so more flowers can grow, so, too, the followers of Jesus spread the Way to more and more and more people.
Soon the seeds of truth were scattering not just from one village to the next, but from country to country. Whole nations were hearing the Good News Paul and the other believers were talking about.

The special thing about Paul's letters is that they continue to spread seeds even today. Christians all over the world can read the words Paul wrote then to his friends. Reading Paul's letters is almost as good as having Paul and Timothy ride up to our house and talk to us in person! Now, as then, we can almost see the two of them, hear the hoofbeats, and feel the excitement.

Even when Paul's enemies were hunting him down, especially in the hard times, Paul's friends knew his words were important Wherever Paul went, he warned the people about the religious leaders.

"They're lying," he told the people. "I know. For years I tried to be good enough by following the rules I couldn't do it. My heart wanted so much to serve God. But I was blind. Now I can see. Jesus really is the Son of God!"

The religious leaden shook their fists at Paul. "He can't call us liars! Kill the traitor,"

The most dangerous place of all was Jerusalem, Paul's former home. Paul knew this. But he also knew Jesus was on his side. After so many years, Paul finally made his last trip through the countryside. He said good-bye to all his friends at the different churches. He knew he had to go to Jerusalem, no matter how dangerous it was.

Once Paul reached Jerusalem, it did not take his enemies long to spring their trap. The religious leaders lied to a mob of people who became so angry, they tried to kill Paul.

"There he is! Grab him!" The crowd went crazy with hatred. Paul's friends tried to protect him, but it was no good. The crowd dragged Paul out of the Temple.

"Stop this Back away!"

"It's the Roman soldiers!" The crowd stopped beating Paul.

"What's this man done? Leave him alone!" The Roman captain had heard there was a riot in the city. He had sent soldiers to stop the fighting. Now he grabbed Paul. "Put this man in chains until we can find out what he's done," he ordered his men.

Then he asked why the crowd wanted to kill Paul. Some people said one thing. Others said something else. "Let us have him, We will give him what he deserves!" The crowd pushed against the Roman soldiers.

"No, you can t have him. We'll take the prisoner back with us," the captain ordered. The mob pressed so hard, though, that the soldiers had to carry Paul to keep him from being torn apart.

Once he was safely out of the crowd's reach, Paul asked twice if he could go back and talk to the religious leaders. "Please, I'm not a criminal Let me talk to the people," he begged the captain.

Both times the crowd went wild with hatred Finally, the Roman captain put him mto prison. He told Paul, "I don't know who you are. I will punish you, though, until you tell me what you've done wrong."

Paul said, "I am a Roman. You cannot beat me without a trial."

These words, "I am a Roman," were very powerful. Paul was right. No one could put him into prison without a trial, not if he was a Roman. The Roman captain knew Paul was right. But he also knew that if he let Paul free, his own people would kill him. Once again he let Paul speak to the religious leaders. For the third time they screamed for Paul's death. This time the Roman captain put him back into prison, for his own good.

Paul had felt the Lord standing by him all this time. Jesus' own Holy Spirit had spoken through Paul, trying to reach the religious leaders. But their hearts were closed. Even Jesus cannot break through a heart which does not want to change.

That night, as Paul slept on the cold, stone floor, he saw the Lord standing right next to him! Be brave, Paul," Jesus told him. "You've done the right thing, telling the people of Jerusalem about Me. Now you must do the same in Rome."

The next morning Paul woke up feeling the peace of God in his heart. "I'll follow You, Jesus, no matter what," he prayed. Paul was ready to do battle.

It was a good thing, too. That same night, forty of Paul's enemies had plotted how they would

ambush Paul the next time he was allowed to speak to the people. Luckily, Paul's nephew heard about the plan and told the Roman captain.

"Get me two hundred men," he ordered a guard. Then he called for Paul and told him about the plot. "I'm not going to take any chances with you. You'll leave tonight under heavy guard. My men will see you to Caesarea. Then you'll be King Agrippa's problem."

Paul escaped on horseback, protected by the Romans from his very own people. But would he ever really be free again?

In Caesarea the Romans kept Paul prisoner for two years. Three different times he went to trial. Paul told his story to two Roman governors, as well as the king.

Even the powerful King Agrippa thought Paul made good sense. He saw no reason to keep him prisoner. He did not want to make the religious leaders angry, though. So, just like the others, King Agrippa did not let Paul go free.

Finally Paul told them, "I am a Roman. That means I can go to Rome and tell the emperor himself how I have done nothing wrong. Take me to Caesar!"

The Romans had no choice. They did as Paul asked. They put him on a ship bound for Rome. Now finally, he was going to the place where Jesus had told Paul he must go.

An armed guard, together with some of Paul's other friends, went with him. The voyage took several months since they kept running into bad weather.

Finally a terrible storm blew the ship up

and down, around and around, as if it were a toy boat. The wind howled and the rain slashed the decks! All the crew thought, "This is the worst storm ever. We're all going to die!"

For two long, horrible weeks the hurricane tossed the ship back and forth It was so dark, no one could even tell when it was night and when it was day!

Finally, Paul told the men, "You must eat. Stay brave. God has shown me that none of US Will die, but you must be strong enough to swim!"

Paul was right. When the ship finally did sink, it was just off the shore of an island. Every one of the crew, together with Paul and his guards, swam to safety.

Safe at last, it did not take long to find another ship headed for Rome. By the time they finally did arrive in Rome, the captam of the guard had seen many times over what a good and honest man Paul was. Paul had bravely led them through their adventures.

Now the captain ordered, "If he must have a guard, all right. But let Paul go where he wants." The other believers welcomed Paul, together with the guard who followed him everywhere.

Paul's battle was not yet over. Paul spoke to the religious leaders. He talked to the important Romans who came to visit him. But no one wanted to anger the religious leaders in Jerusalem by giving Paul his freedom.

For several years Paul was free to live outside the prison. Many people came to hear Paul. He wrote more letters to his friends. But always, there was a Roman soldier standing guard over him.

Just when Paul seemed to have found a little bit of freedom, it was taken away from him again. One last time, Paul's enemies had him thrown into prison There, Paul spent his last years, this time chained to his guard. In jail, he kept writing letters to the friends he had made during his long years of wandering. Up to the very end, Paul never stopped telling people about Jesus.

Just before he was killed, Paul wrote his young friend, Timothy, "How I long to see you. I can still remember how you cried when we last said goodbye. My son, please come and visit soon. I know the end is near. I am ready. I have fought the good fight, I have finished the race."

When Paul died, he left behind the stones of hatred and fear which had so often been thrown at him. He went to heaven There he joined Stephen and all the many others who have chosen to let Jesus change their hearts.

You can find the story of Paul in the New Testament Book of Acts, chapters 9-28. Some of the letters Paul wrote are in the Bible. He wrote to the Romans, Corinthians, Galatians, Ephesians, Philippians, Colossians and Thessalonians, as well as to Timothy, Titus and Philemon.